Before the Presidency: How Donald Trump's Past Shaped America's Present

By

Aren Frost

ISBN (eBook): 979-8-89604-635-6

ISBN (Paperback): 979-8-89604-636-3

ISBN (Hardback): 979-8-89604-637-0

About The Author

Aren Frost is a political analyst and long-form commentator focused on leadership psychology, institutional power, and the evolution of modern political culture. His work explores the intersection between personality and governance, examining how individual temperament shapes public institutions and democratic norms.

Drawing on investigative journalism, historical continuity, and documented testimony from primary sources, Frost approaches political subjects with an analytical lens rather than a partisan one. His writing emphasizes evidence-based evaluation over reactionary interpretation, encouraging readers to examine patterns across time rather than isolated headlines.

In *Before the Presidency: How Donald Trump's Past Shaped America's Present*, Frost traces decades of behavioral continuity to understand how leadership style evolves, hardens, and ultimately influences governance. His work seeks not only to critique, but to contextualize, offering readers tools to engage politics thoughtfully and historically.

Acknowledgments

This book was shaped by many voices, both direct and indirect. While the responsibility for its conclusions rests entirely with me, its development benefited from the insight, criticism, and encouragement of individuals who value rigorous political analysis and honest inquiry.

I am grateful to the journalists, historians, legal scholars, and former public officials whose documented work, interviews, and testimony made evidence-based examination possible. Their commitment to record-keeping and transparency provides the foundation upon which serious political study depends.

My thanks also extend to colleagues and early readers who challenged assumptions, pressed for clarity, and insisted on historical continuity rather than reactionary interpretation. Their questions strengthened the arguments presented here.

To the editorial and research team who assisted in organizing sources, verifying timelines, and maintaining analytical consistency across chapters, I offer sincere appreciation. Precision matters in political writing, and their diligence ensured that evidence remained central.

Finally, I acknowledge the readers – those who approach this subject with strong opinions, and those who approach it with uncertainty. This book was written not to inflame, but to examine. In an era defined by immediacy and polarization, thoughtful engagement is itself an act of civic responsibility.

Table of Contents

PART I – THE TRANSFER OF POWER AND FORMATIVE BUSINESS YEARS

Chapter 1: Taking Control of the Family Business

When we look at Donald Trump's rise, it is tempting to begin with the presidency, the rallies, or the headlines that followed him for years. But if we want to understand who he became in power, we have to start much earlier. That means looking inside the family business where his instincts were first shaped. Long before politics entered the picture, we see the beginnings of a pattern: authority taken rather than earned, rules treated as flexible, and conflict used as a tool rather than something to avoid.

In taking control of his father's real estate operation, Trump was not simply stepping into a successful enterprise. We see him reshaping it in his own image, favoring control over cooperation and image over responsibility. Former business partners, tenants, and legal records describe a young executive who learned quickly that pressure, persistence, and public confidence could overpower restraint or compromise. These early years matter because they reveal something essential: the behaviors that later defined Trump as a political leader were not created by politics. They were learned, reinforced, and normalized in the first arena where he held power.

The Trump Family: Power, Loyalty, and Expectation

Before we examine the business itself, we need to understand the family structure that shaped it. The Trump household was not simply a family unit; it was an ecosystem built around authority, loyalty, and hierarchy. At its center stood Fred Trump, the patriarch, whose expectations defined both success and failure for his children.

Fred Trump and his wife, Mary Anne Trump, raised five children: Maryanne, Fred Jr., Elizabeth, Donald, and Robert. Each occupied a different place in the family hierarchy, but it was clear early on which traits were valued and which were dismissed. Fred Jr., the eldest son, was once seen as the natural successor, but his reluctance to fully embrace his father's ruthless business culture ultimately sidelined him. His struggles and eventual marginalization sent a powerful message within the family: approval was conditional, and weakness, either real or perceived, was not tolerated.

Donald Trump emerged in this environment as the child most willing to mirror his father's intensity, ambition, and confrontational style. Maryanne Trump, who went on to become a federal judge, and the other siblings pursued quieter, more conventional paths. Donald, by contrast, leaned into the family's power structure, aligning himself closely with Fred's worldview. From an early age, we see a family dynamic that rewarded dominance, punished deviation, and treated success not as a shared value, but as a personal conquest.

Fred Trump's Business Philosophy and Operating Style

Fred Trump was not a flashy developer, nor was he interested in public acclaim. His success was built on discipline, scale, and relentless cost control. He focused primarily on large-scale residential housing in Brooklyn and Queens, operating within a tightly managed system that prioritized predictability and leverage over risk-taking. To Fred, business was not about innovation or vision; it was about control.

We see Fred Trump's philosophy clearly in how he treated money, tenants, and government institutions. He was deeply conservative with spending, aggressive in securing public subsidies, and unyielding in disputes. Court records and contemporaneous reporting describe a businessman who viewed regulations as challenges to be navigated rather than obligations to be respected. Legal pressure, delay, and negotiation were tools, not last resorts.

Perhaps most importantly, Fred Trump believed in dominance as a business principle. Contractors were pushed hard, tenants were managed at scale, and disputes were rarely resolved through compromise. Winning mattered more than harmony. This operating style created a culture where confrontation was normalized and accountability flowed upward only when unavoidable.

When Donald entered this world, he did not learn business as a cooperative enterprise. We see him absorbing a lesson that would repeat throughout his life: power belongs to those who press hardest, and survival belongs to those who refuse to concede. Fred Trump's business philosophy did not simply provide Donald with capital or opportunity; it provided a blueprint. One that rewarded aggression, blurred ethical lines, and taught that success is measured not by stability or fairness, but by who walks away standing.

Donald Trump's Assumption of Leadership

When Donald Trump first entered the family business, he did not arrive as its unquestioned leader. His early role was closer to that of an apprentice operating under the long shadow of his father. Fred Trump remained firmly in control, and Donald's initial responsibilities were limited, closely supervised, and often designed to test his temperament as much as his competence. We see a young man eager to prove himself, not through patience or quiet mastery, but through visibility, confidence, and confrontation. From the start, Donald showed little interest in maintaining the cautious, low-profile style that had defined his father's success.

As Donald took on more responsibility, his approach began to diverge sharply from Fred's. Where Fred valued predictability and control, Donald pushed for expansion, attention, and symbolic wins. He sought projects that carried his name, elevated his profile, and signaled authority beyond the confines of the family operation. According to former associates and business records, Donald was quick to assert dominance in meetings, override advisers, and frame decisions as personal victories. This was not merely ambition; it was a deliberate effort to redefine the business around himself rather than operate within an inherited structure.

Donald's rise within the company was accelerated not only by his drive, but by his willingness to embody the traits his father rewarded most. He projected toughness, dismissed caution as weakness, and showed an appetite for risk that set him apart from his siblings. As Fred Trump aged, Donald increasingly positioned himself as the natural heir, not through formal transition alone, but by behaving as though the role already belonged to him. Over time, authority shifted less through paperwork than through presence. Donald became the public face of the enterprise, the negotiator, the self-appointed decision-maker whose confidence often substituted for consensus.

By the time Donald Trump emerged as the dominant figure in the family business, the transition was effectively complete. The company still bore his father's foundations, but its direction, tone, and public identity had changed. We see in this period the early consolidation of habits that would later define his leadership elsewhere: a reliance on force of personality, a tendency to equate control with success, and a belief that prominence itself was proof of legitimacy. The family enterprise did not simply give Donald Trump a platform. It became the first arena in which he learned how to take power, hold it, and make it unmistakably his own.

Early Conflicts with Advisers and Contractors

As Donald Trump began asserting himself inside the family business, conflict was not an occasional byproduct of growth; it became a defining feature of how he operated. We see this most clearly in his early dealings with advisers and contractors, where disagreement quickly turned into confrontation and compromise was treated as defeat. These conflicts were not hidden episodes. They were frequent, documented, and revealing.

One of the earliest and most cited examples involves the construction of Trump Tower in the early 1980s. Contractors and subcontractors later alleged that Trump routinely delayed payments, disputed invoices, or withheld funds altogether. According to court records and reporting by investigative journalists, several firms claimed they were forced into settlements for less than what they were owed rather than endure prolonged legal battles. Former contractors described a pattern in which Trump used the threat of litigation and financial exhaustion as leverage, confident that smaller firms could not afford extended disputes. This pattern is documented in contemporaneous court filings and later examined in detail by journalist Wayne Barrett, who chronicled Trump's business practices over several decades.

We also see early tension between Trump and professional advisers who attempted to impose restraint. Legal aides from this period, quoted in later memoirs and reporting, described a client who resisted caution and viewed legal advice as an obstacle rather than a safeguard. When advisers warned against aggressive tactics or potential exposure, Trump often pushed forward regardless, preferring confrontation over compliance. According to reporting by David Cay Johnston, Trump's approach frequently placed advisers in a reactive role, tasked with defending decisions after the fact rather than shaping them beforehand.

Another notable conflict involved the renovation of Wollman Rink in Central Park. While Trump later promoted the project as evidence of managerial brilliance, records and reporting from the time show disputes over credit, costs, and responsibility. City officials and contractors recalled Trump publicly claiming success while privately disputing payments and scope. The episode reinforced a pattern we see repeatedly:

public triumph paired with private conflict, and visibility prioritized over collaboration.

These early disputes matter because they establish how Trump learned to manage power. We see a businessman who discovered that aggression often worked, that legal pressure could substitute for negotiation, and that reputational dominance could outweigh operational fairness. Former partners and contractors, speaking on the record years later, consistently describe the same dynamic: Trump framed every disagreement as a test of strength, and he expected to win. This approach did not emerge later in politics. It was practiced, refined, and normalized in the earliest years of his leadership within the family enterprise.

What Former Partners and Employees Tell Us

When we listen to people who worked closely with Donald Trump in his early business years, a consistent picture emerges: an executive obsessed with image, intolerant of dissent, and quick to frame disagreement as weakness. These are not isolated impressions. They come from former executives and staff who described their experiences in detail long before politics defined his public persona.

One of the clearest assessments came from former Trump Organization employees who told The Guardian that Trump was intensely self-focused and demanding. As one long-time staffer put it, *"His identity is wrapped around being a winner. He thinks wining solves everything."* Another bluntly summarized the internal atmosphere: *"Donald loves Donald."* These former employees described a leader who equated disagreement with personal attack and loyalty with unquestioning compliance.

Barbara Res, who served in a senior construction role during the Trump Tower build-out, spoke candidly in multiple interviews about the environment she entered. She recalled that Trump was quick to assign blame outward rather than reflect inward when setbacks occurred. This is an approach that pushed advisers and project managers into defensive positions early and often. In one quoted exchange, a colleague noted that issues were treated as personal affronts rather than opportunities to solve problems collaboratively.

Blanche Sprague, another senior executive involved in major Trump projects, offered similar observations. She described periods in which managing Trump could feel "like a nanny job," forced to handle not just professional logistics but also personal grievances about perceived slights or disruptions. Sprague's recounting, such as being paged late at night over trivial matters, highlighted a recurring tolerance for intensity at the expense of normal workplace boundaries.

Other insiders echoed these themes. Project supervisors often noted that Trump's attention to the smallest detail, from terrace alignments to public optics, combined with a reluctance to share or delegate authority, created tension. One former manager explained that even when Trump praised work publicly, behind the scenes he would revisit contracts, challenge estimates, or demand unilateral cuts, reinforcing a pattern of micromanagement merged with aggressive negotiation.

Taken together, these testimonies paint a vivid picture of a leader in constant vigilance over his own narrative, resistant to critique, and prone to interpret challenge as disloyalty. Advisers were not treated as collaborators but as instruments to be pressed into service or dismissed when they failed to conform. Contractors and employees alike learned early on that working for Trump meant navigating a temperament that prized domination over dialogue and victory over long-term partnership. This dynamic did not wait for the presidency to appear; it was visible in the business decisions and interpersonal conflicts of Trump's first major leadership roles.

Preference for Dominance over Collaboration

As Donald Trump gained confidence inside the family enterprise, we begin to see a clear shift in how decisions were made and how authority was exercised. Collaboration was not something he cultivated; it was something he tolerated only when it reinforced his control. From early on, Trump showed a strong preference for unilateral decision-making, often sidelining advisers once their usefulness had passed. Meetings were less about weighing options and more about asserting direction. Input was welcomed only if it confirmed what he had already decided.

Former executives and advisers consistently describe a management environment where questioning Trump's judgment carried consequences. Disagreement was interpreted not as professional engagement but as personal resistance. We see this in how projects were handled: Trump frequently overrode technical advice, demanded changes late in development, and reframed collective work as individual achievement. Contractors and managers learned quickly that collaboration did not protect them – compliance did. This created a culture where people anticipated Trump's reactions rather than offering honest assessments, reinforcing his belief that decisive force mattered more than shared expertise.

Trump's negotiations further illustrate this preference for dominance. Rather than seeking mutually beneficial outcomes, he approached deals as contests with winners and losers. Settlements, concessions, and public credit were framed as proof of strength. When partners pushed back, Trump often escalated the matters using delay, publicity, or legal pressure until resistance weakened. The lesson he appeared to internalize was simple: pressing harder usually worked. Cooperation slowed him down; dominance moved him forward.

What stands out in these early years is how quickly this approach became habitual. Trump did not experiment with collaborative leadership and reject it after failure. He bypassed it almost entirely.

Success, measured in visibility and personal leverage, reinforced his instincts. Each project completed on his terms confirmed the same belief: authority was something to be imposed, not shared. This mindset, formed well before politics entered the picture, would later define how Trump interacted with institutions, advisers, and even allies once he held far greater power.

Power Learned Early

By the end of this chapter, we are left with a clear understanding of where Donald Trump's leadership instincts took shape. His assumption of control within the family business was not a gradual evolution toward shared authority or measured stewardship. It was a decisive shift toward dominance, where pressure replaced persuasion and visibility mattered as much as results. The family enterprise became Trump's first proving ground, teaching him that aggression could substitute for experience, that confrontation often produced compliance, and that winning, even at the cost of relationships, was its own justification.

What we see here is not simply a young businessman finding his footing, but a pattern being set. Early conflicts with advisers and contractors, the sidelining of collaboration, and the elevation of personal authority over institutional process all reinforced a single lesson: power belongs to those who take it and refuse to yield. These habits did not emerge later under the stress of public office. They were learned early, rewarded often, and rarely challenged in ways that forced meaningful change.

As we move into the next chapter, *Manhattan Ambition and the Cult of Visibility*, we follow Trump as he carries these instincts into a much larger arena. No longer confined to the family business, he seeks validation on a public stage, where attention itself becomes a form of power. The shift to Manhattan is not merely geographic; it marks the moment when Trump begins to merge dominance with spectacle, transforming personal ambition into public identity. The traits formed in the family enterprise do not disappear. Instead, they expand, sharpen, and begin to shape a persona that will eventually reach far beyond real estate.

"Born into leverage."

Chapter 2: Manhattan Ambition and the Cult of Visibility

When we leave the family business and follow Donald Trump into Manhattan, we are not just watching a young developer change markets. We are watching a shift in ambition, scale, and self-definition. Manhattan offered something Brooklyn and Queens never could: visibility. It was a stage where success was not measured quietly in balance sheets, but loudly in headlines, skylines, and public perception. For Trump, this was irresistible. Power, he had already learned, was about dominance. Manhattan taught him that dominance could be amplified through spectacle.

In this chapter, we see Trump deliberately step into an arena where attention itself becomes currency. He does not simply want to build; he wants to be seen building. We follow how he leverages political connections, public subsidies, and media coverage to transform high-risk projects into personal statements. Former associates, city officials, and contemporaneous reporting describe a developer who understood early that controlling the narrative could be as important as controlling the property. The move to Manhattan marks the moment when Trump begins to fuse business ambition with personal branding, turning visibility into validation and exposure into power.

This chapter examines how the instincts formed in the family enterprise – dominance over collaboration, confrontation over restraint – find a larger and more rewarding outlet in Manhattan. Here, public attention does more than elevate Trump's profile; it reinforces his belief that success is proven by who commands the spotlight. The cult of visibility that emerges in this period will shape not only his business career, but his political future, teaching him that being talked about is often more powerful than being understood.

Strategic Shift from Outer-Borough Real Estate to Manhattan

When we look at Donald Trump's decision to leave the relative safety of outer-borough real estate and push into Manhattan, we see a move driven as much by psychology as by strategy. Brooklyn and Queens had made the Trump family wealthy, but they could not make Donald Trump famous. For him, Manhattan represented legitimacy, dominance, and public validation. It was the one arena where success would be unmistakable and failure impossible to hide. Choosing Manhattan was not simply an expansion of the business; it was a rejection of the quiet, disciplined model that had defined his father's success.

Outer-borough real estate rewarded patience, scale, and operational control. Manhattan demanded risk, leverage, political navigation, and constant visibility. Trump embraced this difference deliberately. He sought projects that were high-profile, complex, and controversial, because they placed him at the center of attention. According to contemporaneous reporting and later accounts from city officials, Trump understood that Manhattan deals were as much political negotiations as business transactions. Tax abatements, zoning exceptions, and public incentives were not side benefits; they were central to making these projects viable. Trump leaned aggressively into this system, lobbying relentlessly and framing his projects as public goods even when private gain was the primary outcome.

The Commodore Hotel redevelopment near Grand Central Terminal illustrates this shift clearly. The project required navigating city bureaucracy, state authorities, and public financing mechanisms. Trump approached these challenges not with restraint, but with force and confidence, presenting himself as the indispensable figure who could revive a failing property. We see here the early merging of business ambition with personal narrative: Trump positioned the project as a test of his ability, not just a financial transaction. Success would not belong to the company – it would belong to him.

This move also marked a change in how Trump measured achievement. In the outer boroughs, success was steady income and long-term stability. In Manhattan, success was symbolic. Buildings carried his name. Deals generated headlines. Media coverage became part of the return on investment. Trump learned quickly that attention amplified leverage. A project discussed in newspapers and on television gave him negotiating power that balance sheets alone could not provide. Visibility became both shield and weapon.

What matters most about this strategic shift is what it reinforced. Manhattan rewarded the traits Trump had already developed: confidence bordering on bravado, a willingness to confront institutions, and an instinct to dominate negotiations rather than collaborate. Each successful step deeper into Manhattan validated his belief that boldness outweighed caution and that public perception could bend reality in his favor. This was not just a new market. It was a proving ground that confirmed Trump's conviction that power, once taken and displayed openly, tends to protect itself.

The Commodore Hotel Redevelopment: A Political–Business Hybrid

When we examine the Commodore Hotel redevelopment, we are not just looking at a real estate deal. We are looking at an early blueprint for how Donald Trump learned to fuse business ambition with political leverage and how he learned to present private gain as public rescue. This project, more than any other in his early career, shows us how Trump began to operate in the space where money, power, and publicity overlap.

The Commodore was a decaying property near Grand Central Terminal, unattractive to many developers because it required navigating multiple layers of government approval, public financing, and institutional risk. Trump did not shy away from these complications. He sought them out. We see him positioning himself not simply as an investor, but as a savior – someone uniquely capable of reviving a failing landmark. This framing mattered. It allowed him to pursue generous tax abatements and public concessions while portraying the deal as a civic necessity rather than a private opportunity.

Visibility is victory.

What deserves critique here is not the use of public incentives alone, as such tools were common in New York real estate but how Trump leveraged them. He aggressively courted city officials, framed opposition as obstructionist, and treated negotiation as a contest to be won rather than a process of shared accountability. The deal ultimately granted decades-long tax relief that dramatically reduced his financial exposure. Risk was shifted outward, while credit flowed inward. The public absorbed uncertainty; Trump absorbed acclaim.

Throughout the project, Trump worked the media as deliberately as he worked city hall. He made himself inseparable from the redevelopment, ensuring that success would be attributed to his personal will rather than a combination of public financing, partnerships, and favorable conditions. The narrative was simple and self-serving: without him, the Commodore would fail; with him, it would thrive. This framing erased the role of government support and reinforced Trump's growing belief that visibility itself was proof of merit.

The Commodore redevelopment reveals an uncomfortable truth about Trump's operating style. We see a leader who learned early how to extract maximum advantage from public systems while presenting himself as an outsider battling them. He did not treat political institutions as partners in governance, but as tools to be pressured, persuaded, or bypassed. The success of the project validated this approach and taught him a lesson he would repeat for decades: if you control the story, the structure behind the story matters less.

In retrospect, the Commodore Hotel was not just Trump's entry into Manhattan. It was his entry into a hybrid world where business success depends on political access and political narratives are shaped to serve personal ambition. The instincts he refined here like personalizing success, externalizing risk, and dominating the narrative would not remain confined to real estate. They would follow him into every arena he entered next, including the one he would later claim was broken beyond repair: politics itself.

Use of Public Incentives and Personal Lobbying

As Donald Trump pushed deeper into Manhattan, we see him relying less on conventional market strength and more on his ability to extract advantage from public systems. Public incentives were not supplements to his deals; they were foundational. Tax abatements, zoning accommodations, and favorable financing terms became tools Trump pursued aggressively and personally. This was not delegated work. We see him inserting himself directly into negotiations with city and state officials, treating access as leverage and persistence as a substitute for consensus.

The Commodore Hotel redevelopment again serves as the clearest example. Trump secured a long-term tax abatement that dramatically reduced the project's risk while preserving its upside. City officials later acknowledged that without these concessions, the deal would not have been viable. Trump understood this dynamic well. Rather than minimizing public support, he reframed it as evidence of his negotiating brilliance. Years later, he would state plainly, **"I love tax breaks,"** presenting government incentives not as shared civic tools but as trophies won through forceful bargaining.

What stands out in contemporaneous reporting is how personally Trump handled these efforts. He did not rely solely on lawyers or intermediaries. He lobbied directly, pressed relentlessly, and framed his projects as urgent public necessities. According to accounts from city officials at the time, Trump often positioned himself as the only figure capable of delivering results, implying that resistance to his terms would result in visible failure. This approach narrowed the space for genuine negotiation and replaced it with pressure.

We also see Trump pairing lobbying with narrative control. While public incentives shifted financial risk away from him, Trump worked diligently to ensure the public story emphasized his courage and vision. The role of government was downplayed; his role was magnified. In interviews and promotional material, Trump spoke of "saving" projects and "reviving" neighborhoods, language that obscured how deeply these deals depended on public cooperation. The message was consistent: success flowed from his will, not from institutional partnership.

This pattern deserves critique because it reveals how Trump learned to treat public systems as adversaries to be exploited rather than structures to be respected. Incentives were not part of a social contract; they were spoils of negotiation. Personal lobbying was not about persuasion; it was about endurance and dominance. Each successful extraction reinforced Trump's belief that institutions bend under pressure and that public accountability can be neutralized through confidence and repetition.

By mastering this approach early, Trump internalized a dangerous lesson: access equals entitlement, and persistence justifies outcome. The use of public incentives and personal lobbying in Manhattan did more than advance his career. It taught him that power, once obtained, could be leveraged repeatedly with little consequence, as long as the narrative remained firmly under his control.

Early Signs of Entitlement and Confrontation when Challenged

As Donald Trump's profile grew in Manhattan, so did his sensitivity to resistance. What begins to stand out in this period is not simply ambition or confidence, but a developing sense of grievance whenever his authority was questioned. Challenges, whether from city officials, journalists, contractors, or competitors, were rarely treated as routine disagreements. We see them reframed as personal attacks, evidence of unfair treatment, or proof that others were conspiring to block his success.

When deals stalled or criticism emerged, Trump's response was often immediate and combative. Rather than adjusting strategy or acknowledging limits, he escalated. Public pushback was met with public counterattack. Private negotiation gave way to confrontation. Contemporaneous reporting shows Trump reacting sharply to negative press, calling reporters directly, disputing facts aggressively, and insisting that any unfavorable coverage was biased or dishonest. The substance of the criticism mattered less than the perceived insult to his authority.

Entitlement also becomes visible in how Trump spoke about access and outcomes. He increasingly portrayed success as something he deserved rather than something contingent on cooperation or restraint. When public officials resisted his terms or questioned his demands, Trump framed their actions as incompetence or obstruction. We see this clearly in disputes over tax abatements, design approvals, and timelines, where compromise was treated as capitulation and delay as betrayal. The assumption underlying these reactions was consistent: if Trump wanted a result, resistance was illegitimate.

Former associates and advisers later described how this mindset affected internal dynamics as well. Warnings were interpreted as disloyalty. Hesitation was read as weakness. Those who questioned Trump's assumptions found themselves marginalized or replaced. Over time, this reinforced a feedback loop: only voices that affirmed his sense of grievance and entitlement remained close, while dissent was pushed out. Trump's worldview narrowed, and confrontation became not just a tactic, but a reflex.

These early signs matter because they reveal how Trump learned to convert challenge into fuel. Opposition did not prompt reflection; it intensified resolve. Criticism did not produce recalibration; it justified escalation. By the time he left Manhattan's development battles behind, Trump had already internalized a powerful belief: that he was perpetually wronged, uniquely capable, and justified in meeting resistance with force. This combination – grievance sharpened by entitlement and expressed through confrontation – would later become central to how he operated on a far larger stage.

Media Cultivation as a Core Business Tool

As Donald Trump's ambitions expanded in Manhattan, we begin to see media attention move from a useful accessory to a central pillar of his business strategy. Trump did not treat the press as a passive observer of success; he treated it as an instrument for creating success. Visibility was not a byproduct of achievement. It was a tool used to manufacture leverage, intimidate opponents, and reinforce his authority in both public and private negotiations.

From early on, Trump understood something many developers ignored: perception could move faster than reality. A project praised in headlines gained momentum regardless of its underlying risk. A reputation for boldness could pressure lenders, officials, and partners into compliance. Trump actively cultivated journalists, especially tabloid reporters and real estate columnists, feeding them stories that elevated his image as a decisive, larger-than-life dealmaker. According to contemporaneous accounts, he was a constant presence on the phone, calling reporters directly, correcting stories, disputing criticism, and ensuring that his name stayed in circulation.

What distinguishes Trump from his peers is how deliberately he blurred the line between publicity and truth. He did not merely promote completed successes; he hyped intentions, projections, and future possibilities as though they were already established facts. Announcements became events. Promises became proof. If a deal faltered, the narrative was adjusted rather than abandoned. Media coverage, once secured, created a sense of inevitability that often outpaced the actual state of the project. Trump learned that once a story took hold, it could become self-reinforcing.

We also see Trump using media attention as a weapon. Critical coverage was not tolerated quietly. Journalists who questioned him were confronted, accused of bias, or frozen out. Trump challenged facts aggressively, often repeating his version of events until it dominated the conversation. This behavior established an early pattern: truth was something to be contested publicly until submission or fatigue set in. The goal was not accuracy but dominance of the narrative space.

Inside the business, this reliance on media altered decision-making itself. Projects were evaluated not only on financial terms, but on their headline potential. Trump favored deals that could elevate his profile even if they carried outsized risk. His name became inseparable from the enterprise, and the enterprise increasingly existed to serve the name. Former associates later described how media moments were prioritized over operational stability, reinforcing Trump's belief that attention equaled success and obscured weakness.

"How did we do?"

Perhaps most consequential was how media cultivation shaped Trump's sense of accountability. Positive coverage validated him; negative coverage radicalized him. Rather than prompting reassessment, criticism was treated as hostile action. This hardened Trump's instinct to fight, exaggerate, and repeat. The press was no longer a mirror reflecting performance; it was an arena to be conquered. Winning coverage mattered more than earning trust.

By the end of this period, Trump had internalized a powerful and dangerous lesson: reality could be negotiated if the story was strong enough. Media cultivation had become inseparable from his business model, reinforcing his preference for spectacle over substance and confrontation over correction. This was not accidental or incidental. It was learned behavior, refined through repetition, and rewarded consistently. When Trump later entered politics, he did not need to adapt to a media-driven environment. He had already built his career around mastering it.

Visibility as Validation, Conflict as Identity

By the end of Trump's Manhattan ascent, something more than a business strategy had taken hold. Media cultivation was no longer just a tool for advancing deals; it had become the mechanism through which Trump understood himself and his success. Attention validated him. Praise confirmed his instincts. Criticism hardened his resolve. Over time, visibility stopped being a means to an end and became the end itself. The louder the spotlight, the more legitimate his authority felt, regardless of outcomes beneath the surface.

What matters here is not simply that Trump learned how to use the media, but how deeply that use shaped his psychology. Constant exposure rewarded exaggeration, punished restraint, and trained him to experience challenge as attack. Public affirmation replaced internal reflection. Narrative control substituted for accountability. Each cycle of attention reinforced a belief that dominance in perception was equivalent to dominance in reality.

As we move into the next part of the book, the focus shifts inward, from what Trump did to what these experiences did to Trump. The pressures of high-risk deals, public scrutiny, and relentless self-promotion did not leave him unchanged. They sharpened traits already present: grievance, entitlement, and a compulsion to confront rather than concede. The next section traces this psychological journey, examining how repeated reinforcement, survival under pressure, and constant validation shaped a temperament that would later collide with institutions far more consequential than the New York press or real estate market. What began as a strategy would, over time, become a mindset, and eventually, a governing style.

PART II – EXCESS, COLLAPSE, AND PSYCHOLOGICAL HARDENING

Chapter 3: The 1980s Expansion and the Performance of Wealth

By the time we enter the next phase of Donald Trump's career, we are no longer watching a developer trying to break into Manhattan. We are watching a man who has tasted visibility and wants more of it. The projects grow larger, the risks grow higher, and the image grows louder. This chapter explores a critical transformation: Trump does not just expand his business portfolio, he expands the performance of himself.

In the 1980s, success in America was increasingly tied to spectacle – bigger towers, grander entrances, louder declarations of wealth. Trump did not resist this culture. He embraced it and amplified it. We see him shift from building properties to building a persona. The gold-plated surfaces, the towering signage, the bold proclamations of "the best" and "the biggest" were not aesthetic accidents. They were psychological signals. Wealth was not simply accumulated; it was displayed, curated, and weaponized.

As we move through this chapter, we examine how expansion became intertwined with excess, and how excess became central to Trump's identity. Former associates describe a leader who equated scale with strength and visibility with legitimacy. The larger the deal, the more it validated him. The grander the presentation, the more it silenced doubt. This was not merely branding. It was a feedback loop in which public perception reinforced personal conviction.

At the same time, risk began to mount. Heavy leverage, ambitious ventures, and aggressive borrowing pushed the boundaries of sustainability. But rather than tempering ambition, each headline seemed to encourage escalation. The performance of wealth began to matter as much as wealth itself. In this environment, success was no longer just financial—it was theatrical.

This chapter sets the stage for understanding how image, risk, and ego fused during Trump's most flamboyant business years. What we see here is not only expansion, but the deepening of a belief: that projecting power can substitute for possessing it, and that the appearance of invincibility can hold reality at bay, at least for a time.

Trump's Deliberate Public Staging of Success

When we look at Trump Tower, we are not simply looking at a building. We are looking at a statement. Completed in 1983 on Fifth Avenue, the tower was designed not just to generate revenue but to project dominance. From the reflective glass façade to the cascading indoor waterfall and gold-toned finishes, everything about the structure was intended to communicate scale, luxury, and inevitability. Trump did not just want to construct a skyscraper. He wanted to construct an image of himself.

We see this clearly in how Trump attached his name to the building in bold, oversized lettering. The branding was not subtle. It was declarative. In an era when many developers operated behind corporate titles, Trump placed himself at the center of the property's identity. The message was unmistakable: this was not merely a project financed by a company; it was the embodiment of a man. Success would not belong to an organization. It would belong to Donald Trump.

The interior staging reinforced this narrative. Marble surfaces, polished brass, mirrored finishes, and a grand atrium created an atmosphere meant to overwhelm. Visitors did not just enter a commercial building; they entered a spectacle. The tower's retail spaces, luxury apartments, and corporate offices were marketed as symbols of elite access. Trump positioned himself as the curator of that access. Buying into the building meant buying into the aura.

Former associates later described how deeply Trump involved himself in presentation details. From design choices to press coverage, he treated every element as part of a larger performance. Launch events, promotional tours, and media interviews were choreographed to elevate both the property and the persona behind it. The tower's success in attracting attention became self-reinforcing. Coverage of the building elevated Trump; Trump's publicity elevated the building.

What deserves scrutiny here is not the ambition of the project, but the deliberate conflation of structure and identity. Trump Tower functioned as a stage on which Trump could perform wealth and authority. It blurred the line between asset and advertisement. Financial viability mattered, but symbolic victory mattered more. The tower allowed Trump to present himself as already triumphant, regardless of the underlying financial mechanics supporting the venture.

We also see in this period the intensification of Trump's belief that spectacle could override skepticism. Critics who questioned the sustainability of the financing or the excess of the design were dismissed as lacking vision. The building's visual impact silenced many doubts. For Trump, the lesson was clear: if you build something big enough and promote it loudly enough, perception can outrun scrutiny.

Trump Tower was more than a real estate achievement. It was a turning point in how Trump understood power. He learned that architecture could serve narrative, that branding could magnify influence, and that public staging could harden reputation. The building did not just change Manhattan's skyline. It solidified Trump's conviction that success, once displayed boldly enough, becomes difficult to challenge, even when the foundations beneath it are far more fragile than they appear.

Blurring the Line between Corporate Brand and Personal Identity

As Trump Tower rose over Fifth Avenue, something else rose with it: the deliberate merging of Donald Trump's personal identity with the corporate identity of his business. This was not accidental branding. It was a calculated fusion. The company did not simply own assets; the assets existed to elevate the name. And the name, large, metallic, and unmistakable, became the product.

We see this shift clearly in how the Trump Organization was presented to the public. Press releases, interviews, and marketing materials consistently centered on Donald himself rather than the operational team behind the projects. Executives, architects, financiers, and contractors faded into the background. The narrative simplified everything into a single figure: Trump as visionary, Trump as dealmaker, Trump as guarantor of excellence. The corporation became an extension of his persona rather than an independent structure with its own governance and accountability.

This blurring carried strategic advantages. If the brand was inseparable from the man, then success amplified his authority beyond the limits of any single project. But it also carried deeper consequences. Financial performance, public reputation, and personal ego became intertwined. A criticism of a building was interpreted as a criticism of Trump himself. A legal dispute involving a property became a personal affront. When identity and enterprise merge, every challenge feels existential.

Former associates have described how this fusion shaped internal culture. Decisions were often evaluated based on how they would reflect on Trump personally rather than on long-term corporate stability. Projects that enhanced visibility were prioritized over those that offered quiet profitability. The brand demanded constant expansion, constant affirmation. To maintain the illusion of continuous ascent, the company had to behave as though momentum was permanent.

We also see how this merging of self and corporation complicated accountability. When things went well, Trump claimed personal credit. When ventures faltered, responsibility was often dispersed or externalized – market conditions, partners, lenders, or regulators were blamed. The corporate structure absorbed risk, but the personal brand sought insulation. This dynamic allowed Trump to project invincibility even during periods of financial strain.

The deeper issue is psychological as much as strategic. By tying his identity so tightly to the brand, Trump reinforced a worldview in which image equaled worth. Growth was not only financial expansion; it was validation. Any contraction, economic or reputational, became intolerable. This heightened sensitivity to perception would later shape how he responded to criticism in every arena he entered.

In blurring the line between corporation and self, Trump did more than create a powerful brand. He eliminated the buffer that typically separates leader from enterprise. There was no institutional shield, no independent identity beyond his own. The company existed to serve the persona, and the persona required constant elevation. What began as a branding strategy evolved into something far more rigid: a personal mythology that demanded reinforcement at all costs.

Internal Volatility and Fear-Driven Loyalty

As Trump's projects grew in scale and visibility, so did accounts of instability inside his organization. Former executives and senior advisers have described an environment defined not by steady leadership, but by volatility. Including rapid mood shifts and public praise followed by private criticism, and a constant demand for personal loyalty. What emerges from these accounts is not merely a high-pressure workplace, but a culture shaped by fear and unpredictability.

Barbara Res, who oversaw construction of Trump Tower, later described Trump's management style as highly personal and reactive. In interviews, she said that when problems arose, "he would scream and yell and blame people," creating an atmosphere where executives worked defensively rather than collaboratively. Res explained that Trump "never accepted responsibility," a pattern she observed repeatedly during disputes over cost overruns or delays. Her recollections suggest a leader who equated error with betrayal and treated operational setbacks as personal insults.

John O'Donnell, former president of Trump Plaza Hotel and Casino in Atlantic City, offered a similarly blunt assessment in his book *Trumped!* He wrote, "The Donald was always looking over your shoulder… He wanted you to know he was the boss." O'Donnell also described Trump's deep sensitivity to criticism, stating that Trump was "thin-skinned" and prone to retaliation if he felt slighted. According to O'Donnell, loyalty mattered more than expertise, and executives who disagreed with Trump risked marginalization or dismissal.

Jack O'Donnell (no relation to John O'Donnell), who also worked within the casino operations, described a leadership culture in which public humiliation was a tool. In interviews following his departure, he explained that Trump would elevate individuals quickly but discard them just as fast if they failed to meet his expectations. This unpredictability fostered compliance rather than honest feedback. Executives learned that survival depended less on strategic judgment and more on aligning visibly with Trump's viewpoint.

Even those who remained loyal for years acknowledged the volatility. In reporting compiled by investigative journalists, former Trump Organization employees described meetings where decisions changed abruptly and directives were issued impulsively. One executive told reporters that working for Trump required "anticipating his mood" rather than following a structured plan. The absence of consistent process made authority intensely centralized. Approval flowed through Trump personally, reinforcing dependence.

These testimonies collectively paint a picture of fear-driven loyalty. Employees did not simply respect Trump's authority; they navigated it carefully. Praise was often public and effusive, but it could vanish overnight. Criticism, when delivered, was blunt and personal. This dynamic ensured that dissent rarely traveled upward. Instead, executives adapted themselves to Trump's temperament, filtering information in ways that protected him from contradiction.

What we see here is not isolated temperament, but the shaping of a leadership model. Volatility became a mechanism of control. Loyalty became synonymous with agreement. Internal instability reinforced Trump's dominance, because uncertainty increased dependence. Executives who might otherwise have challenged strategy instead focused on maintaining proximity and avoiding conflict.

These patterns are critical because they foreshadow the leadership style that would later move from boardrooms to the national stage. The same volatility described by business executives, like rapid reversals, personal loyalty tests, and intolerance of dissent, would later appear in political appointments, cabinet turnover, and public feuds. The internal culture of the Trump Organization was not an anomaly. It was an early rehearsal for how power would be exercised when the stakes became immeasurably higher.

Early Use of Public Humiliation

As we trace Donald Trump's rise through the 1980s and early 1990s, one management pattern becomes difficult to ignore: public humiliation as a tool of control. This was not accidental or occasional. It was a recurring tactic used to reinforce hierarchy, discourage dissent, and remind those around him who held ultimate authority.

Former executives in Atlantic City describe scenes where subordinates were reprimanded openly rather than privately. John R. O'Donnell, who served as president of Trump Plaza Hotel and Casino, recounted in his book *Trumped!* that Trump would "berate executives in front of others" when displeased, often over performance metrics or minor operational issues. O'Donnell wrote that Trump had "a need to dominate every situation," and that criticism was often delivered in a way designed not simply to correct but to intimidate. According to O'Donnell, the message was clear: loyalty and submission were safer than independent judgment.

Barbara Res, who oversaw construction of Trump Tower, described similar dynamics in interviews. She recalled that when projects ran into difficulty, Trump would publicly assign blame rather than privately address solutions. In one interview, she explained that Trump was quick to "scream and yell" in front of teams when angered. These outbursts were not just emotional reactions; they reinforced the hierarchy. When executives watched a colleague singled out, the lesson was immediate and unmistakable.

We also see evidence of this pattern in how Trump handled contractors and vendors. Several lawsuits and lien disputes from the 1980s document situations where contractors claimed they were pressured aggressively over payment disagreements. While the financial details varied, the broader theme was consistent: Trump was willing to use reputational pressure and public positioning to assert dominance. Contractors who pushed back risked being publicly framed as incompetent or overcharging. The imbalance of power worked in his favor.

What makes these examples significant is not merely their frequency, but their psychological impact. Public humiliation creates a chilling effect. It narrows communication. It discourages honesty. Instead of fostering problem-solving, it produces compliance. Executives learned to anticipate Trump's moods, to frame bad news carefully, and sometimes to withhold dissenting views altogether. The workplace became reactive rather than strategic.

Critically, this tactic also fed Trump's public image. Strength was demonstrated not through quiet leadership, but through visible assertion. Dominance, once displayed, reinforced his authority both internally and externally. By humiliating subordinates publicly, Trump reinforced the narrative that he alone controlled outcomes. It was a performance of command, and it carried consequences.

These early episodes show us more than temper. They reveal a leadership philosophy rooted in intimidation rather than collaboration. Public humiliation was not simply emotional excess; it functioned as a management strategy. And as we move forward, we begin to see how this method, effective in silencing boardroom dissent, would later resurface in political rallies, press conferences, and cabinet dismissals on a much larger stage.

When Image Replaced Restraint

By the end of this chapter, we are no longer looking at a businessman trying to establish credibility. We are looking at a figure who has fully embraced excess as identity and dominance as method. Trump Tower was not just a building. It was a declaration. The gold surfaces, the towering signage, the constant press coverage – these were not aesthetic flourishes. They were signals. They told the world that power must be seen to be believed, and that belief itself could substitute for stability.

Inside the organization, the culture hardened. Volatility became routine. Loyalty became survival. Public humiliation reinforced hierarchy. Executives learned to align rather than question. Contractors learned to settle rather than fight. The company did not operate through steady institutional process; it revolved around the temperament of one man. What began as ambition evolved into performance. And performance, repeated often enough, became reality.

But beneath the spectacle, risk was accumulating. Heavy borrowing, aggressive expansion, and the relentless need to maintain the appearance of triumph created structural strain. The image of invincibility required constant reinforcement. Success had to be projected even when foundations trembled. Trump had built not only towers, but a persona that demanded perpetual ascent. There was no room for visible retreat.

As we move into the next chapter, *High Stakes and Hard Landings*, we confront what happens when performance collides with financial gravity. The 1980s boom would give way to the harsh realities of overleveraged ventures and mounting debt. For the first time, Trump's model of spectacle would be tested by forces he could not dominate through publicity alone. The collapse that followed would not simply threaten his fortune; it would shape his psychology. Crisis would either humble him or harden him. The question we now explore is which path he chose, and what that choice reveals about the leader he would eventually become.

Chapter 4: Financial Crisis and Survival Instincts

Up to this point, we have watched Donald Trump expand, project strength, and build a public image of unstoppable ascent. Manhattan validated him. Trump Tower elevated him. The media amplified him. But every model built on leverage eventually faces a test. In the late 1980s and early 1990s, that test arrived with force.

This chapter marks a turning point. The deals grew bigger. The borrowing grew heavier. Casinos, airlines, and luxury ventures stretched the limits of sustainability. For a time, the performance of wealth masked the underlying fragility. But when market conditions shifted and revenues fell, perception alone could not service debt. The carefully staged image of invincibility collided with financial reality.

What makes this period critical is not simply that Trump encountered crisis—many developers did. What matters is how he responded. Faced with near insolvency, strained relationships with lenders, and the threat of personal ruin, Trump did not retreat quietly. Instead, we see survival instincts sharpen. Negotiations became more aggressive. Responsibility shifted outward. Public messaging intensified.

The financial crisis of this era did more than endanger Trump's empire. It shaped his operating philosophy. Pressure reinforced his belief that confrontation works. Brinkmanship became strategy. Risk was not abandoned; it was recalibrated. The experience hardened rather than humbled him.

In this chapter, we examine how close Trump came to collapse, how he maneuvered through it, and what the episode reveals about his resilience and his refusal to accept limits. Because in moments of crisis, leadership character is exposed. And what emerged here would later reappear under very different, far more consequential pressures.

Casino Failures, Airline Ventures, and Extreme Leverage

By the late 1980s, Donald Trump was no longer operating within the relative safety of high-profile Manhattan real estate. He had moved into industries that required massive upfront capital, sustained cash flow, and disciplined long-term management. Instead of moderating risk, he escalated it. Casinos in Atlantic City and the acquisition of an airline were not incremental expansions. Instead, they were debt-fueled bets that depended on constant growth and favorable economic conditions. When those conditions shifted, the structure began to crack.

Trump's casino empire in Atlantic City grew rapidly. Trump Plaza opened in 1984, followed by Trump Castle in 1985, and most notably the Taj Mahal in 1990. The Taj Mahal, promoted as "the eighth wonder of the world," was financed heavily through high-interest junk bonds. According to contemporaneous reporting and financial disclosures, the project carried nearly $1 billion in debt. The burden was enormous, and the revenue projections required to sustain it were optimistic at best. Within a year of opening, the Taj Mahal was struggling to meet interest payments.

In 1991, the Taj Mahal filed for Chapter 11 bankruptcy protection. It was not an isolated incident. Trump Plaza and Trump Castle would also undergo restructurings. By 1992, multiple Trump casino properties had entered bankruptcy proceedings. Public records and financial reporting from the time show that Trump had personally guaranteed substantial portions of the debt, placing his broader empire at risk. Analysts described the leverage levels as extreme. The structure depended less on operational strength and more on continued borrowing and favorable refinancing.

The airline venture followed a similar pattern. In 1988, Trump purchased the Eastern Air Shuttle, rebranding it as Trump Shuttle. The acquisition, valued at approximately $365 million, was financed largely through borrowed money. Trump again relied on debt to acquire a prestige asset that aligned with his image of luxury and success. The airline, however, faced stiff competition and economic headwinds. Revenue projections fell short, and by 1990 the venture was faltering. In 1992, control of the airline passed to creditors. The brand survived briefly, but the enterprise did not.

What connects these ventures is not simply failure; it is the scale of exposure relative to underlying stability. Trump's model during this period prioritized spectacle and scale over prudence. The Taj Mahal's marble interiors and lavish opening events reinforced the public image of wealth, but they masked a fragile financial foundation. The airline's gold-plated fixtures and high-end marketing conveyed exclusivity, yet they could not compensate for operational deficits.

Financial journalists at the time reported that by the early 1990s, Trump's personal debt obligations exceeded $900 million, with total business liabilities reaching several billion dollars. Banks that had once courted him began reassessing their exposure. Lenders formed oversight committees. Credit terms tightened. For the first time, Trump was no longer the dominant negotiator – he was dependent on creditor patience.

Critically, these failures did not produce a public admission of overreach. Instead, Trump framed the restructurings as strategic maneuvers rather than collapses. Bankruptcy was described as business technique. Debt was portrayed as leverage mastered rather than leverage miscalculated. The narrative rarely centered on misjudgment. It centered on resilience.

This period reveals an important pattern. Trump did not stumble into financial distress because of a single unpredictable event. The crisis was rooted in an operating philosophy that equated boldness with superiority and treated debt as an extension of confidence. Extreme leverage magnified gains during boom years, but it also amplified vulnerability when conditions turned. The spectacle could not outrun arithmetic indefinitely.

The casino failures and airline collapse mark the first large-scale collision between Trump's cultivated image of invincibility and measurable financial limits. The question was no longer whether he could command attention. It was whether he could survive consequences. And survival, as we will see, became the defining instinct of this era.

Near Insolvency in the Early 1990s

By the early 1990s, the image of relentless ascent had collided with financial reality. The combination of overleveraged casino properties, a struggling airline venture, and broader economic slowdown left Donald Trump facing a crisis that threatened not only his business empire, but his personal solvency. This was not a minor downturn. It was a moment when lenders openly questioned whether he could survive.

"Risk is just another headline."

At the center of the crisis was debt – massive, layered, and increasingly unmanageable debt. Financial reporting from the period documented that Trump had personally guaranteed hundreds of millions of dollars in loans. Estimates at the time placed his personal exposure at over $900 million, with total liabilities tied to his businesses reaching several billion dollars. Much of this debt carried high interest rates, particularly the junk bonds used to finance the Taj Mahal casino. When revenues failed to meet projections and the economy softened, the cash flow required to service that debt evaporated.

The Taj Mahal's bankruptcy filing in 1991 signaled that the crisis was no longer containable. But it was only one piece of a larger unraveling. Trump Plaza and Trump Castle required restructuring. Trump Shuttle was losing money and ultimately transferred to creditors. Even flagship properties such as the Plaza Hotel in New York struggled under heavy debt loads. At one point, analysts described Trump's empire as overextended beyond sustainable limits, dependent on continued refinancing rather than operational strength.

Banks that had once competed for Trump's business began to treat him as a liability. According to contemporaneous reporting, major lenders, including Citibank, Chase Manhattan, and others, formed creditor committees to manage their exposure. Trump was reportedly placed on strict spending allowances for personal expenses, a dramatic reversal for someone who had built his public identity around opulence. The spectacle of gold-plated interiors contrasted sharply with the private negotiations happening behind closed doors.

What makes this period particularly revealing is how close Trump came to collapse. There were serious discussions among creditors about forcing asset sales and imposing tighter controls. Trump's name, once synonymous with triumph, was increasingly associated with overreach. Financial publications questioned whether his empire had been built more on borrowed capital than durable value.

Yet even at this low point, Trump resisted acknowledging defeat. Publicly, he minimized the severity of the crisis. Privately, he negotiated aggressively, persuading lenders that his personal brand still held value.

Banks ultimately chose restructuring over liquidation, not necessarily out of confidence in his management, but because forcing bankruptcy could have triggered greater losses for themselves. Trump survived in part because he was "too exposed to fail" for the institutions that had financed him.

Critically, the near-insolvency did not appear to temper his appetite for risk. Instead, it reinforced a lesson: debt could be renegotiated, lenders could be pressured, and survival could be spun as victory. Bankruptcy, rather than being an admission of failure, became framed as a strategic tool. The crisis did not dismantle his belief in dominance; it reshaped it. He learned that brinkmanship, when combined with persistence and publicity, could carry him through even systemic collapse.

The early 1990s marked the most financially vulnerable period of Trump's career. The empire wavered. Credit tightened. Control slipped. But rather than redefine his philosophy, Trump emerged hardened. Insolvency had not humbled him. It had confirmed his conviction that survival, no matter how attained, was proof of strength.

Negotiations with Banks under Threat of Total Collapse

When Donald Trump's financial structure began to fracture in the early 1990s, the balance of power shifted sharply. For the first time in his career, he was not negotiating from a position of expansion. He was negotiating for survival. The debts tied to his casinos, airline, and flagship properties had reached levels that made default a real possibility. Lenders were exposed. So was he. What followed was not a quiet restructuring. It was a prolonged, high-stakes standoff between a borrower on the brink and banks determined to limit their losses.

By 1990 and 1991, Trump had personally guaranteed hundreds of millions of dollars in loans. Reports at the time estimated his personal exposure at roughly $900 million, with overall corporate liabilities in the billions. The Taj Mahal alone carried nearly $1 billion in high-interest junk bond debt. When cash flow faltered, bondholders and banks faced the prospect of massive write-downs. Citibank, Chase Manhattan, Manufacturers Hanover, and Bankers Trust were among the major institutions deeply entangled in Trump's obligations.

Rather than accept collapse, Trump turned to aggressive renegotiation. According to financial reporting from the period, creditor banks formed a steering committee to coordinate discussions and avoid chaotic liquidation. Trump argued that forcing bankruptcy would damage not only his empire but the banks themselves. He framed his personal brand as a valuable asset – one that could still generate revenue if stabilized. In essence, he presented himself as both the problem and the solution.

One of the most revealing aspects of these negotiations was the extent to which Trump's personal lifestyle became a bargaining chip. Banks reportedly imposed limits on his spending, restricting his monthly personal allowance while restructuring agreements were hammered out. Credit lines were frozen. Oversight increased. For a figure who had built his public image around unlimited wealth, this was a sharp reversal. Yet publicly, Trump downplayed the severity, describing restructurings as routine business maneuvers rather than emergency measures.

The outcome of these talks was not a single sweeping rescue but a series of restructurings. Debt was extended, interest terms were adjusted, and Trump surrendered partial ownership stakes in certain properties. In some cases, lenders converted debt into equity. In others, they agreed to temporary relief in exchange for tighter financial supervision. The Taj Mahal entered Chapter 11 bankruptcy in 1991, allowing bondholders to swap debt for equity while Trump retained a reduced but visible role.

Critically, banks did not act purely out of confidence in Trump's management. Many analysts noted that lenders were motivated by self-preservation. Forcing liquidation during a downturn could have triggered deeper losses and destabilized broader portfolios. Trump's projects were large enough that their failure would ripple outward. In that sense, he benefited from being deeply entangled within major financial institutions. The cost of letting him fall outright was higher than negotiating.

What stands out in these negotiations is Trump's instinct for brinkmanship. Rather than concede vulnerability, he pressed the argument that he remained indispensable to the properties' future success. He leveraged his public persona as collateral, convincing lenders that the Trump name still held promotional value. Survival was framed not as rescue, but as proof of resilience. In later interviews, Trump would describe this period as evidence of his deal-making prowess, reinforcing the narrative that he had outmaneuvered the system rather than narrowly escaped ruin.

The negotiations under threat of total collapse reveal something fundamental about Trump's operating style. Faced with financial disaster, he did not retreat into caution. He escalated into persuasion, pressure, and narrative control. He transformed a near-insolvency into a story of strategic restructuring. The banks preserved their capital. Trump preserved his name. And the lesson absorbed was powerful: even when the numbers turn against you, confidence and confrontation can bend outcomes in your favor, at least enough to survive.

Bankers Describing Trump Under Pressure

When Donald Trump's empire began to wobble in the early 1990s, the people who saw him most clearly were not reporters or competitors. Instead, they were bankers. These were the lenders who had extended enormous lines of credit, often based as much on Trump's perceived aura of success as on hard collateral. When the numbers stopped working, those same bankers had to decide whether to cut him loose or keep him afloat. Their descriptions of Trump during this period are revealing and not flattering.

William D. Cohan, in his book *The Last Tycoons*, recounts how Wall Street bankers viewed Trump during the crisis years. One senior banker described him as a borrower who "never admitted a mistake," even when projections collapsed. According to Cohan's reporting, lenders quickly recognized that Trump would resist any arrangement that publicly framed him as defeated. Protecting the image was as important to him as restructuring the debt. In negotiations, he emphasized his personal brand value, arguing that the Trump name itself was an asset the banks could not afford to damage.

'Balance is optional.'

A former Citibank executive, quoted in multiple financial retrospectives, explained that dealing with Trump required constant recalibration. The banker described Trump as intensely combative when challenged, often shifting blame to market conditions, advisers, or bond structures rather than acknowledging misjudgment. The executive's assessment was blunt: Trump negotiated "as though perception could substitute for cash flow." Under pressure, he leaned harder into confidence rather than pulling back into concession.

Journalistic accounts from the period also captured how close to collapse the situation had become. According to reporting in *The New York Times* in the early 1990s, Trump's personal guarantees placed him on the brink of insolvency, forcing lenders to intervene collectively. One banker involved in the steering committee later recalled that Trump's main argument was simple: "You don't want me to go bankrupt." It was not a plea for forgiveness; it was a reminder of shared exposure. If he fell, they fell with him.

Former lenders have also described Trump's reliance on brinkmanship. Rather than approach negotiations as collaborative restructurings, he treated them as contests of endurance. A senior banker, reflecting years later, noted that Trump's strategy was to push creditors to recognize that liquidation would be more painful for them than compromise. The implication was clear: he would not concede easily, and forcing him out could trigger losses they were unwilling to accept.

Critically, bankers did not describe a humbled borrower. They described a resistant one. Trump did not arrive at the table acknowledging overreach. He arrived insisting that his continued involvement was essential. Even after bankruptcies were filed for several casino properties, he framed the outcome publicly as savvy use of legal tools. To creditors, however, the episode demonstrated that Trump's appetite for leverage had far exceeded sustainable limits.

The bankers' perspective exposes the gap between narrative and reality. While Trump later characterized the early 1990s as evidence of his deal-making genius, many of the lenders involved saw a different picture: a highly leveraged borrower whose survival depended less on strategic brilliance than on the banks' unwillingness to absorb deeper losses. He was not rescued because he was invincible. He was preserved because dismantling him would have been expensive.

Under pressure, Trump's negotiating style did not soften, it intensified. He deflected responsibility, emphasized his brand value, and pressed creditors to accept restructuring as the least damaging option. The experience reinforced a lesson he would carry forward: if you are large enough, loud enough, and deeply entangled enough, collapse becomes negotiable.

Blame-Shifting in Crisis

When Donald Trump's financial empire came under severe strain in the early 1990s, the pressure did not produce public introspection or visible recalibration. Instead, it appeared to sharpen traits that had already been present—defensiveness, resentment toward critics, and a consistent tendency to shift responsibility outward. Crisis did not soften Trump's posture. It hardened it.

Throughout the restructuring period, Trump repeatedly framed his financial distress as the product of external forces. The broader recession, rising interest rates, Atlantic City competition, and unfavorable bond markets were emphasized as primary causes. While those factors were real, what was noticeably absent was sustained public acknowledgment of overleveraging or miscalculated projections. The heavy reliance on junk bonds for the Taj Mahal, the premium paid for the Plaza Hotel, and the debt-financed airline purchase were rarely described by Trump as strategic errors. Instead, he portrayed the downturn as a temporary storm weathered through resilience.

Financial journalists at the time noted that Trump's public messaging rarely matched the severity of private negotiations. Even as banks imposed tighter controls and creditors negotiated equity swaps, Trump described bankruptcies as "technical" or strategic. The word "failure" was avoided. The narrative shifted toward survival as victory. In later interviews, he characterized the period as evidence of his negotiating brilliance rather than as a cautionary tale about excess.

Former associates from that era described a leader increasingly sensitive to criticism. According to executives quoted in business reporting, Trump reacted strongly to negative coverage, calling reporters directly to dispute details and accuse them of bias. Legal advisers reportedly spent substantial time managing reputational fallout as much as financial exposure. The pattern suggests that criticism during crisis was not processed as feedback; it was treated as attack.

Internally, defensiveness translated into sharper scrutiny of subordinates. Former employees have described a culture in which setbacks were attributed to advisers, managers, or shifting market conditions rather than leadership decisions. Blame moved downward or outward, rarely upward. This created an environment where executives became cautious in delivering bad news, reinforcing a cycle of filtered information and delayed correction.

Resentment also appears to have deepened during this period. Trump frequently expressed frustration with bankers who tightened terms, portraying them as shortsighted or ungrateful. He argued publicly that he remained an asset to lenders and that they had benefited from association with his projects. The implication was consistent: obstacles were imposed unfairly by others, and his intentions remained justified.

What makes this moment pivotal is not simply that Trump survived financial collapse, but how he interpreted that survival. Instead of viewing the crisis as evidence that limits matter, he appeared to internalize a different lesson: that systems bend under pressure, that criticism can be countered with repetition, and that persistence ultimately overrides admission. The experience reinforced confrontation as a default response.

Crisis often reveals character by stripping away insulation. In Trump's case, the early 1990s exposed a pattern that would later resurface in politics, externalizing fault, attacking critics, and reframing setbacks as proof of strength. Financial distress did not moderate his instincts. It entrenched them.

Survival without Surrender

By the end of this chapter, we are left with a defining moment in Donald Trump's evolution – not just as a businessman, but as a personality shaped by pressure. The early 1990s were not a minor setback. They were a near-collapse. Casinos entered bankruptcy. The airline slipped away. Personal guarantees threatened to wipe out the image of limitless wealth he had worked so carefully to construct. For a brief period, the mythology cracked.

But what followed was not surrender. It was survival.

Trump did not emerge from this crisis chastened or restrained. He emerged convinced that endurance equals victory. Debt could be renegotiated. Bankruptcy could be reframed. Lenders could be pressured. Criticism could be dismissed. Instead of internalizing caution, he internalized a more dangerous lesson: if you push hard enough and refuse to concede publicly, collapse becomes negotiable.

The financial crisis did not reduce his appetite for dominance. It intensified his defensiveness. It deepened his resentment toward critics. It strengthened his instinct to shift blame outward and claim credit inward. Survival reinforced the belief that confrontation works. And once reinforced, that belief became part of his operating code.

As we move into the next chapter, we begin to examine the psychological consequences of this era. What does it mean for a leader to experience near-ruin and come away feeling vindicated? How does repeated survival without public accountability shape one's view of risk, truth, and power? The next stage of Trump's journey is not just about rebuilding finances. Instead, it is about rebuilding identity. Because after surviving collapse, Trump did not simply recover. He recalibrated. And that recalibration would influence every arena he entered next.

Chapter 5: Litigation as Strategy

By the time we reach this stage of Donald Trump's career, a pattern has become unmistakable. When challenged, he does not retreat. He counters. When cornered, he does not concede. He escalates. In business disputes, financial strain, or reputational threats, Trump repeatedly turned to one tool with particular confidence: the legal system. Lawsuits were not merely defensive shields. They were instruments of pressure.

This chapter examines how litigation became embedded in Trump's operating philosophy. Courtrooms were not simply places where conflicts were resolved; they were arenas where leverage could be applied, opponents could be exhausted, and narratives could be shaped. Over decades, Trump and his companies were involved in thousands of legal actions as plaintiff and defendant. The volume alone suggests something more than coincidence. It reflects a strategy.

We will look at how Trump used legal threats to renegotiate contracts, delay obligations, and shift bargaining power. We will also examine how he framed lawsuits publicly, as proof of strength, as retaliation against unfair treatment, or as tactical maneuvers rather than disputes over conduct. Former legal advisers and business partners have described a leader who viewed the courtroom not as a last resort but as a negotiating table with sharper edges.

The critical question in this chapter is not whether Trump had the right to defend his interests—any business leader does. The question is how often litigation replaced collaboration, and how the repeated use of lawsuits shaped his worldview. Because once legal confrontation becomes habitual, it changes how power is exercised. It normalizes conflict. It encourages brinkmanship. And it reinforces a belief that institutions exist to be leveraged rather than respected.

As we move forward, we examine litigation not as isolated episodes, but as a consistent method – one that reveals how Trump learned to turn legal pressure into a form of dominance.

Trump's Reliance on Lawsuits

By the 1980s, litigation was no longer an occasional response for Donald Trump. It had become part of his operating rhythm. Court filings were not simply reactions to disputes; they were often extensions of negotiation. Over time, a pattern emerged: when challenged financially, contractually, or reputationally, Trump frequently turned to legal action not just to resolve conflict, but to gain leverage, intimidate opponents, or buy time.

"When challenged, escalate."

Public records show that Trump and his companies have been involved in thousands of legal cases over several decades, both as plaintiffs and defendants. While high-profile developers inevitably encounter lawsuits, what distinguishes Trump is the frequency with which he initiated legal action. Contractors who claimed unpaid bills were often met with countersuits. Business partners who disputed terms faced prolonged litigation. Journalists and critics were threatened with defamation suits, even when those cases had limited chance of success.

The practical effect of this strategy was often delay. Litigation can stall payment obligations, extend negotiations, and exhaust smaller opponents who lack comparable financial resources. Several contractors from Trump Tower and Atlantic City projects alleged that they were pressured into accepting reduced settlements after months of legal wrangling. The message was implicit: fighting would be expensive, and Trump had greater capacity to endure prolonged disputes. Whether every claim against him was valid is secondary to the pattern – legal confrontation became a negotiating tactic.

We also see this approach in Trump's use of defamation threats. Reporters who published unfavorable stories often received letters from Trump's attorneys demanding retractions. Even when lawsuits did not proceed fully, the threat itself carried weight. Legal pressure created friction and uncertainty, signaling that criticism would not go unanswered. This tactic reinforced Trump's broader instinct to treat opposition as something to be suppressed rather than debated.

Former legal advisers have described how Trump preferred aggressive responses over compromise. In accounts from former counsel and reporting by investigative journalists, Trump is portrayed as a client who believed that counterattacking legally projected strength. Rather than view lawsuits as costly last resorts, he treated them as demonstrations of resolve. The courtroom became another arena in which dominance could be displayed.

Critically, reliance on litigation also insulated Trump from immediate accountability. Legal processes move slowly. Cases can take years to resolve. During that time, public attention often shifts elsewhere. Even when settlements occurred, they frequently did so without admissions of wrongdoing. This allowed Trump to claim victory or vindication, regardless of the underlying dispute's merits.

The cumulative effect of this strategy was cultural as well as financial. Within his organization, executives understood that disputes would likely escalate to legal confrontation. Opponents learned that conflict would be prolonged. Over time, this normalized a combative posture. Lawsuits were not anomalies, becoming the expected tools of business.

What emerges from this record is a leader who viewed the legal system less as a neutral arbiter and more as a strategic resource. Litigation offered intimidation. It offered delay. It offered leverage. And for Trump, those qualities were often more valuable than resolution.

Legal Aides Describe Impulsive Decisions

If we want to understand how Donald Trump approached conflict, we have to listen closely to the lawyers who represented him. Legal advisers occupy a unique position. They see the raw reaction before the press statement, the immediate instinct before the strategic framing. And many of those who have spoken publicly describe a client driven less by measured calculation than by impulse, especially when ego or reputation were involved.

Michael Cohen, who served for years as Trump's personal attorney and fixer, has described a decision-making process that was often reactive and emotionally charged. In congressional testimony and in his memoir, Cohen portrayed Trump as someone who would demand immediate action against critics, sometimes instructing legal threats before fully assessing the consequences. According to Cohen, Trump's first response to negative coverage was frequently, "Sue them," even when the legal merits were thin. Whether or not a case ultimately proceeded, the instinct was confrontation, not deliberation.

John Dowd, who represented Trump during the early stages of the special counsel investigation years later, provided a similar portrait of impulsiveness under pressure. While Dowd's tenure occurred during Trump's presidency, his reflections reinforce a long-standing pattern. Dowd told reporters that managing Trump required constant effort to prevent public or legal escalations that could worsen the situation. He indicated that Trump was often eager to respond quickly and aggressively, sometimes against legal advice. Though this example comes from a later period, it aligns with accounts from earlier business years: impulse first, strategy second.

George Ross, a longtime executive vice president at the Trump Organization and a lawyer by training, has described Trump as someone who thrived on confrontation and rarely hesitated to initiate it. In interviews and in his book *Trump-Style Negotiation*, Ross acknowledged Trump's instinct to push hard and move fast, even when legal complexity required patience. While Ross often framed these traits as strengths, his accounts reveal a leader who valued speed and pressure over caution.

Former in-house counsel and outside attorneys have also described the challenge of restraining Trump when disputes escalated. According to reporting from the 1980s and 1990s, Trump frequently called for lawsuits or countersuits as immediate responses to setbacks. Lawyers were often tasked with either executing these directives or persuading him to reconsider. The tension between legal prudence and personal reaction became a recurring theme.

What emerges from these accounts is not simply aggressiveness, but impulsiveness tied to ego. Legal action was often demanded not after careful weighing of risk, but after perceived insult. Advisers who urged restraint sometimes found themselves sidelined. The legal system became an extension of Trump's temperament, which was swift, confrontational, and personal.

Critically, impulsive decision-making under legal stress can have long-term consequences. It increases costs, prolongs disputes, and narrows options. Yet for Trump, the immediate display of force appeared to outweigh those considerations. The act of striking back mattered. The signal of strength mattered. And over time, this reinforced a worldview in which delay, escalation, and spectacle became normal responses to challenge.

When we connect these descriptions back to his earlier financial crises and public battles, a pattern becomes clear. Trump did not approach legal conflict as a quiet technical matter. He approached it as a personal contest. And in contests, impulse often replaced restraint.

Escalation Pattern

As we examine Donald Trump's long history of legal conflict, one pattern appears again and again: escalation in public, resolution in private. Disputes were often amplified loudly, through lawsuits, countersuits, press statements, or aggressive rhetoric, only to conclude later through settlements that received far less attention. The cycle itself became a strategy.

"Double down."

The escalation phase was typically immediate and visible. When contractors sought unpaid compensation, Trump's companies frequently responded with legal defenses that challenged the quality of work or the validity of claims. When journalists published unfavorable stories, letters from attorneys or threats of defamation suits often followed quickly. The message during this stage was unmistakable: resistance would be met with force. Even when the underlying dispute involved relatively modest sums, the response signaled willingness to fight.

However, many of these confrontations did not culminate in definitive courtroom victories. Instead, they concluded quietly. Contractors who filed liens or lawsuits over nonpayment often reached confidential settlements. Trump University litigation, though far later in his career, provides a high-profile example of the same pattern: years of aggressive defense and public denunciation of plaintiffs were followed by a multimillion-dollar settlement without admission of wrongdoing. The escalation created pressure; the settlement ended the immediate risk.

In earlier decades, similar patterns appeared in business disputes tied to Trump Tower and Atlantic City projects. Vendors alleged withheld payments. Trump's companies disputed the claims. Litigation dragged on. Ultimately, many cases resolved out of court. Settlements are not admissions of guilt, but the consistency of the pattern is telling: public confrontation reinforced dominance, while private settlement managed exposure.

This approach offered several advantages. First, escalation discouraged smaller opponents who lacked resources for prolonged legal battles. Second, even if a settlement required compromise, it often occurred without dramatic public consequence. By the time disputes were resolved, media attention had shifted. The narrative remained largely intact. Trump could continue projecting strength while minimizing reputational damage.

Critically, the pattern also reinforced Trump's worldview. If escalation forced compromise, then escalation appeared effective. If settlement occurred without visible defeat, then confrontation seemed low-cost. Over time, this created a feedback loop. Legal battles were not deterrents; they were tools. The objective was rarely moral vindication. It was leverage.

This cycle—attack first, settle later—reveals how Trump blended spectacle with pragmatism. The public phase established toughness. The private phase contained risk. Together, they allowed him to sustain an image of unyielding strength while navigating the practical realities of legal vulnerability. It was not about winning every case. It was about controlling the impression of victory.

As we step back from individual lawsuits and look at the broader arc, we see that litigation became less about justice and more about choreography. Escalation was performance. Settlement was damage control. And the repetition of this pattern shaped how Trump would later approach disputes far beyond the boardroom.

Legal Conflict as Rehearsal for Political Combat

When we step back and look at Donald Trump's decades of legal battles, a larger pattern emerges. The courtroom was not just a place where disputes were settled. It became a training ground. The habits formed in business litigation—attack first, concede little, frame criticism as hostility, and stretch conflict over time—closely resemble the tactics he later carried into politics.

In business disputes, Trump learned that escalation reshapes the battlefield. A lawsuit shifts attention from the original accusation to the spectacle of the fight. The focus moves from "Did he overpromise?" to "Who will win?" That reframing is powerful. It turns scrutiny into competition. When Trump later entered the political arena, he applied the same instinct. Allegations were not answered quietly; they were countered loudly. Critics were not debated; they were challenged, threatened, or dismissed as biased actors with ulterior motives.

The legal strategy of delay also became politically useful. In business, prolonged litigation bought time. In politics, drawn-out investigations, appeals, and procedural challenges achieved similar ends. Legal complexity created confusion. Confusion diluted accountability. The longer a controversy remained unresolved, the more public attention shifted to the next flashpoint. Trump had already learned that time itself can be leverage.

We also see continuity in how Trump personalized conflict. In business lawsuits, disputes over contracts or payments often became framed as attacks on him personally. In politics, institutional oversight, whether from courts, journalists, or legislative bodies, was similarly portrayed as persecution. The language changed arenas, but the psychology remained intact. Opposition was rarely institutional or structural; it was hostile and targeted.

Former advisers have noted that Trump approached political investigations with the same posture he had adopted toward business litigation: fight aggressively, question the legitimacy of the process, and signal unwavering defiance. The message to supporters mirrored the message once sent to contractors and lenders: strength lies in resistance. Compromise looks like weakness.

Most importantly, legal combat normalized perpetual confrontation. When a leader spends decades viewing conflict as routine and victory as survival, politics becomes simply a larger stage for the same performance. The press becomes another opposing counsel. Congressional oversight resembles adversarial negotiation. The objective shifts from resolving disagreement to overpowering it.

What began as a business tactic hardened into a governing style. Litigation trained Trump to treat institutions not as frameworks to operate within, but as arenas to dominate. The courtroom taught him that aggressive counterattack energizes supporters and unsettles opponents. It taught him that settlement, if necessary, can be quiet and delayed. And it taught him that public posture often matters more than private concession.

In that sense, Trump's years of legal conflict were not interruptions to his career. They were preparation. They rehearsed the very instincts of escalation, personalization, and defiance that would define his approach to political combat on a national scale.

Conflict as a Way of Life

By the end of this chapter, litigation no longer appears as a series of isolated disputes. It reveals itself as a mindset. For Donald Trump, the courtroom was never merely a place of defense. It was a platform for assertion. Lawsuits were used to intimidate, to delay, to reframe, and to exhaust. Escalation became reflex. Settlement became strategy. The pattern repeated often enough that it ceased to be reactive and became foundational.

What stands out is not simply the volume of cases, but the philosophy behind them. Legal conflict was rarely approached as a problem to be resolved quietly. It was treated as a contest to be dominated publicly. Threaten first. Counterattack loudly. Extend the fight. Then, when necessary, close the matter discreetly. This method reinforced Trump's belief that strength lies not in consensus, but in confrontation.

The psychological effect of this repetition cannot be overlooked. Years of turning criticism into combat conditioned Trump to see opposition as illegitimate and institutions as obstacles rather than guardrails. The legal system became something to leverage rather than respect. Accountability became something to manage rather than accept. Conflict was no longer situational—it was constant.

As we move forward in the book, we begin to see how this culture of perpetual legal combat merged with public ambition. The skills honed in courtrooms and negotiation rooms would soon find a much larger arena. Because once conflict becomes habit, stepping into politics does not require reinvention. It simply requires amplification. And for Trump, amplification was never a challenge—it was an opportunity.

PART III – REINVENTION AND THE MEDIA FEEDBACK LOOP

Chapter 6: Licensing the Name, Limiting the Risk

After surviving financial collapse, Donald Trump did not abandon ambition. But he did adjust the mechanics behind it. The era of extreme leverage and high-stakes ownership had nearly destroyed him. What followed was not retreat, it was recalibration. If direct exposure to debt had proven dangerous, then distance from risk became the next strategic move.

This chapter examines how Trump shifted from building and owning to branding and licensing. Instead of pouring borrowed money into new ventures, he increasingly sold the use of his name. Towers, hotels, products, and developments around the world began carrying the Trump brand, even when he did not own the underlying assets. The structure was different, but the visibility remained. Risk was diluted. Image was preserved.

We see here a crucial transformation. The Trump name itself became the primary commodity. It was marketed as a guarantee of luxury, exclusivity, and success. Licensing allowed Trump to expand globally without absorbing the same level of financial exposure that had nearly bankrupted him. The burden of construction and financing often fell on partners, while the brand delivered the headline.

Critically, this shift did not reduce the centrality of ego or spectacle. If anything, it intensified it. When the name becomes the product, protecting that name becomes paramount. Reputation is no longer symbolic, it is revenue. The brand must appear untarnished, powerful, and in demand. This model allowed Trump to project global influence while limiting personal vulnerability.

In this chapter, we explore how licensing reshaped Trump's business empire, how it insulated him from direct operational risk, and how it further blurred the line between performance and substance. Because once a name becomes the asset, the next step is inevitable: the brand no longer depends on buildings alone. It begins to transcend them.

Shift from Ownership to Branding and Licensing

After the near-collapse of the early 1990s, we see Donald Trump make one of the most consequential adjustments of his career. He did not stop expanding. He changed how he expanded. Instead of relying primarily on debt-heavy ownership, he increasingly relied on licensing agreements and branding partnerships. The asset was no longer just real estate. It was his name.

This shift was both strategic and self-protective. Direct ownership required borrowing, exposure to market fluctuations, and responsibility for operational performance. Licensing required far less capital. Under the licensing model, outside developers financed and built projects while paying Trump for the right to use his brand. The financial risk shifted outward. The visibility remained centered on him.

We begin to see this model take shape in international hotel and residential developments during the 1990s and 2000s. Trump-branded properties appeared in cities where he held limited or no ownership stake. In many cases, the Trump Organization's role focused on branding, marketing input, and occasionally management services rather than direct capital investment. Public filings and reporting from that era document how licensing fees and management contracts became increasingly important revenue streams.

This was not simply a financial maneuver. It was a psychological recalibration. Ownership had nearly destroyed him. Branding allowed him to maintain the appearance of empire without carrying its full weight. The Trump name became scalable in a way physical property could not be. It could be affixed to towers, golf courses, consumer goods, and eventually media ventures. The brand detached from bricks and mortar and attached itself to perception.

Critically, this transition did not eliminate controversy. Some licensing deals became entangled in disputes when projects underperformed or faced legal complications. Because Trump's name was prominently displayed, the distinction between ownership and licensing was often blurred in public understanding. While legal structures limited his direct liability, reputational exposure remained. Yet even here, the structure offered insulation. If a partner's project faltered, Trump could point to contractual boundaries.

We also see how licensing reinforced Trump's emphasis on image over infrastructure. When the brand is the product, presentation becomes paramount. Promotional materials, glossy renderings, and launch events carried disproportionate importance. The success of a deal was often measured by the expansion of the brand's footprint rather than long-term operational durability. Expansion itself became evidence of relevance.

From a critical standpoint, this shift reveals a pattern of adaptation without introspection. Trump did not appear to abandon high visibility or ambition. He modified the architecture of exposure. Instead of stepping back from risk entirely, he redistributed it. Instead of leveraging debt to build assets, he leveraged reputation to monetize influence. The lesson absorbed from the early 1990s was not caution – it was insulation.

By moving from ownership to branding and licensing, Trump preserved the spectacle while reducing personal financial vulnerability. He learned that a name, if aggressively marketed, could be more flexible than a building. And once the name became central, the stage was set for something even larger than global real estate expansion: the conversion of brand recognition into political capital.

Maintaining Dominance while Avoiding Exposure

One of the most consequential outcomes of Trump's post-crisis recalibration was this: he found a way to shrink his personal financial exposure without shrinking his public footprint. After nearly losing everything to overleveraged ownership, he adjusted the structure of his empire so that risk moved outward while recognition stayed firmly attached to him.

Licensing and management agreements allowed Trump to preserve the image of expansion while transferring much of the financial burden to partners and investors. In earlier years, if a tower underperformed or a casino faltered, Trump's balance sheet absorbed the shock. Under the new model, outside developers financed construction, secured loans, and bore operational volatility. Trump provided branding, marketing input, and the symbolic guarantee of luxury. The legal architecture insulated him. The signage elevated him.

We see how effective this shift was in the proliferation of Trump-branded projects worldwide during the late 1990s and 2000s. Towers rose in cities where Trump had little direct capital invested. The public saw expansion. The financial exposure, however, was often limited to licensing revenue streams. If a project struggled, Trump could maintain distance through contractual boundaries, even as his name remained on the façade. The dominance was visual; the liability was contractual.

This restructuring also altered the perception of scale. Because the brand traveled farther than owned assets ever could, Trump appeared larger than his balance sheet alone might justify. The number of projects bearing his name created the impression of unstoppable growth. Yet behind the scenes, many of these ventures required minimal upfront capital from him. Dominance became an aesthetic, which was measured in global presence and headline value rather than direct ownership percentages.

Critically, this reduction of exposure did not moderate Trump's appetite for projection. If anything, it reinforced it. The less personal capital he had tied to each deal, the freer he was to pursue visibility aggressively. The brand could stretch across industries, such as real estate, golf, and consumer products, without replicating the financial vulnerability of the early 1990s. Risk was diluted. Recognition was amplified.

There is a deeper implication here. By decoupling personal liability from public prominence, Trump refined a model of influence that depended more on perception than on operational depth. Power appeared expansive, even if structural control was limited. The distinction between ownership and association blurred in the public eye. And for Trump, the blurring was beneficial.

This strategy reveals something fundamental about his evolution. The crisis had not reduced his need for dominance. It had taught him how to preserve it more efficiently. He learned that insulation can coexist with spectacle. That one can project empire while limiting exposure. And that in the modern marketplace, and eventually in modern politics, perceived strength often matters more than measurable stake.

Partners on Trump's Need for Control without Accountability

As Trump shifted from ownership to branding and licensing, former partners and executives began describing a consistent dynamic: Trump sought visible control over projects while structuring arrangements that limited his exposure when problems arose. The pattern, according to multiple accounts, was dominance in presentation paired with insulation in liability.

Jack O'Donnell, former president of Trump Plaza Hotel and Casino, wrote in *Trumped!* that Trump demanded authority over major decisions and public messaging, even when he delegated operational detail. O'Donnell described a leader who "wanted total loyalty" and who frequently intervened in matters large and small, but who was quick to distance himself when financial strain surfaced. The structure, as O'Donnell portrayed it, preserved Trump's personal credit while shifting operational risk to managers and lenders.

George Ross, a longtime executive vice president at the Trump Organization, offered a more sympathetic but revealing view in *Trump-Style Negotiation*. Ross acknowledged that Trump insisted on maintaining final say and visible ownership of outcomes, even when his formal stake was limited. The brand, Ross explained, required tight control over how projects were presented to the public. Yet licensing structures often left development financing and operational burdens to outside partners.

Business partners in several international Trump-branded developments echoed similar concerns in later reporting. In some projects where disputes emerged, such as failed hotel ventures or stalled developments, partners noted that Trump's organization had strong contractual protections limiting direct liability. While Trump's name dominated marketing materials, formal ownership and financial exposure were often narrower than the public understood. This allowed him to retain brand prominence while distancing himself from setbacks.

One notable example involved Trump University, where Trump was heavily involved in promotional messaging but structured the enterprise through corporate layers. When litigation followed, he publicly defended the program aggressively while legal defenses emphasized corporate separation. The case eventually settled for $25 million without admission of wrongdoing. The episode reinforced what former associates had long suggested: Trump sought visibility in success but relied on legal structure in crisis.

Even outside formal partnerships, former employees described a culture in which accountability flowed downward. Barbara Res has stated in interviews that Trump often demanded visible control but resisted acknowledging fault when projects encountered difficulty. Decisions were centralized. Praise was personalized. Responsibility, when necessary, was distributed elsewhere.

What emerges from these testimonies is not simply a leader protective of his interests—that is common in business—but one deeply invested in preserving authority while minimizing vulnerability. Trump's name functioned as the centerpiece of each venture, yet the contractual architecture frequently insulated him from the full consequences of failure. Control remained visible. Accountability became negotiable.

Critically, this combination shaped Trump's later approach to leadership. The habit of claiming ownership over success while compartmentalizing risk did not end with branding deals. It became a defining feature of how he navigated institutions and controversy. Partners saw it in boardrooms. The public would later see it on a much larger stage.

Reinforcement of Ego-Driven Decision-Making

As Donald Trump transitioned from high-risk ownership to brand licensing, one psychological pattern deepened rather than diminished: ego-driven decision-making. If the early financial crisis had nearly undone him, the branding era seemed to confirm something far more seductive – that the strength of his name alone could command markets, loyalty, and attention. The business model shifted, but the decision-making center did not. It remained intensely personal.

When a brand becomes inseparable from an individual, choices stop being purely strategic and start becoming symbolic. Projects were often evaluated not just on long-term profitability, but on how prominently they would display the Trump name. Expansion into new markets carried reputational value beyond financial metrics. The larger the signage, the more global the footprint, the more it affirmed the narrative of dominance. Business became affirmation.

Former executives and advisers have described a culture in which decisions frequently revolved around personal pride. If a partner proposed changes that diluted the visibility of the Trump brand, resistance followed. If media coverage suggested overextension, the response was not quiet recalibration but public insistence on continued growth. Ego, not restraint, guided trajectory. Success reinforced confidence; criticism intensified defiance.

Licensing further amplified this pattern. Because Trump often had less capital at stake, there were fewer structural barriers to expansion. The lower personal exposure created more room for reputational risk-taking. If a project faltered financially, the brand might suffer reputational strain, but the underlying loss often belonged to someone else. This imbalance encouraged bold announcements and ambitious branding exercises that fed perception without demanding equal operational accountability.

We also see ego shaping how setbacks were interpreted. When disputes arose in branded projects, Trump frequently emphasized the strength of the name rather than acknowledging operational shortcomings. The narrative consistently returned to his personal excellence as a dealmaker. Over time, repetition of that narrative appeared to harden into belief. Confidence moved beyond projection into conviction.

Critically, ego-driven decision-making narrows feedback loops. When identity and enterprise merge, disagreement feels like disloyalty. Advisers may hesitate to challenge assumptions. Partners may soften objections. The leader, increasingly insulated from contradiction, relies on instinct reinforced by affirmation. In Trump's case, years of media attention and branding success created a self-sustaining cycle in which visibility validated decision-making, even when underlying fundamentals were complex.

The reinforcement of ego during this period is significant because it shaped how Trump interpreted authority itself. If personal instinct had carried him through collapse and branding had amplified his influence, then reliance on that instinct seemed justified. The more the brand expanded, the more it affirmed the central belief: that his judgment alone could dictate outcomes.

By the end of this phase, ego was not an accessory to strategy. It was embedded within it. Decisions flowed through a personal lens, filtered by perception, and reinforced by the absence of meaningful consequence. That mindset would not remain confined to real estate and branding. It would eventually enter a realm where ego-driven choices carried consequences far beyond balance sheets.

The Brand Becomes the Shield

By the end of this chapter, we see that Donald Trump did not retreat from ambition after his near-collapse in the early 1990s. He reengineered it. Ownership gave way to branding. Direct exposure gave way to contractual insulation. The name became the primary asset, scalable across cities and industries without replicating the financial vulnerability that had once threatened to destroy him.

But this was more than a business adjustment. It was a psychological consolidation. Licensing allowed Trump to project expansion while limiting accountability. Success was personalized. Risk was redistributed. Control remained highly visible, even when operational responsibility rested elsewhere. The structure reinforced a powerful lesson: dominance does not require ownership; it requires perception.

In insulating himself financially, Trump also insulated his ego. The brand's growth affirmed his instincts. The reduced exposure minimized immediate consequence. Decision-making increasingly revolved around image, affirmation, and symbolic victory. Each new project bearing his name became proof, not just of market demand, but of personal validation.

"If it shines, sign it."

What we are witnessing here is the final refinement of a model that blends spectacle with insulation. The Trump name could now travel faster and farther than any physical asset. It could generate revenue without direct liability. It could command attention without proportional risk. And once that lesson was fully internalized, a larger possibility came into view.

As we move into the next chapter, we step into the media age in its fullest form. The brand that once depended on buildings now finds a new platform—television. If licensing expanded Trump's reach geographically, television will expand it culturally. The performance of authority will no longer be limited to boardrooms or lobbies. It will enter living rooms across America. And in doing so, it will prepare the ground for something even bigger than business.

Chapter 7: Television and the Manufacture of Authority

By the time Donald Trump entered television, he had already built towers, survived collapse, and transformed his name into a global brand. But television offered something none of those arenas could fully deliver: mass intimacy. Real estate created spectacle. Licensing created scale. Television created familiarity. It brought Trump directly into American homes, week after week, in a format that allowed him to perform authority rather than merely claim it.

This chapter marks a critical transition. Trump no longer needed buildings to project power. On screen, he could embody it. As host of *The Apprentice*, he was presented as the decisive executive, the ultimate judge of competence, the embodiment of success. The boardroom scenes were tightly staged. The language was sharp and final. "You're fired" became not just a catchphrase, but a cultural symbol of command.

What matters here is not simply that Trump became a television personality. It is how television reshaped his public identity. Millions of viewers encountered a curated version of him—disciplined, commanding, unchallenged. The complexities of debt restructurings, licensing structures, and quiet settlements disappeared behind the performance. Authority was edited, scored with music, and broadcast as fact.

In this chapter, we examine how reality television manufactured a version of Trump that felt authentic but was carefully constructed. We explore how the medium amplified traits he had long cultivated—dominance, confidence, and confrontation—while filtering out instability and vulnerability. Television did not just enhance his brand. It recast him as a national figure whose authority appeared natural, decisive, and unquestioned.

Because once authority is performed consistently enough, it begins to feel real. And for Trump, television did more than polish reputation; it helped him rehearse leadership in front of a mass audience. The stage was no longer a lobby or a licensing agreement. It was prime time.

The Apprentice as Reputation Rehabilitation

By the early 2000s, Donald Trump's public image was uneven. He was known, certainly but not universally admired. The financial turmoil of the 1990s, the casino bankruptcies, and persistent questions about leverage had complicated the mythology of effortless success. He remained visible in New York real estate and branding circles, but his reputation was no longer untouchable. Then came *The Apprentice*.

When NBC launched *The Apprentice* in 2004, it did more than introduce a reality competition show. It reintroduced Donald Trump to a national audience in a controlled, highly edited environment. On screen, he was not the overleveraged developer negotiating with banks. He was the decisive executive presiding over a polished boardroom, evaluating ambitious contestants and delivering firm judgments. The chaos of Atlantic City was replaced with the symbolism of Manhattan authority.

Television offered Trump something powerful: narrative control through production. Every episode reinforced the same image. Trump sat at the head of the table. Contestants competed for his approval. Advisors flanked him but did not overshadow him. When he declared "You're fired," the moment was edited for maximum impact—music swelled, cameras tightened, silence lingered. Authority was dramatized. The audience saw a man in command.

Critically, *The Apprentice* reframed Trump's business history. The complexities of debt restructuring and bankruptcy were absent. What viewers absorbed instead was a weekly lesson in leadership as dominance. Trump was portrayed as a billionaire tycoon whose instincts were sharp and whose standards were uncompromising. The show's format reinforced a simple narrative: Trump builds winners and discards weakness. It simplified decades of mixed outcomes into a digestible myth of consistent success.

The ratings success of the show amplified this rehabilitation. Millions watched. Trump's name returned to the center of popular culture—not as a businessman who survived crisis, but as a symbol of executive authority. Interviews, magazine covers, and talk show appearances followed. The television persona began to overwrite the financial history. For a generation of viewers, Trump was not the casino magnate who filed for Chapter 11; he was the decisive boss who rewarded competence and punished failure.

From a critical standpoint, *The Apprentice* did not simply restore Trump's visibility—it reshaped memory. It replaced complexity with clarity. It turned a checkered financial narrative into a story of mastery. And because television reaches emotionally before it reaches analytically, the impression proved durable. Repetition normalized it. Authority performed weekly became authority assumed.

In retrospect, the show functioned as reputation rehabilitation at scale. It polished the brand, reintroduced it to a broader audience, and aligned it with confidence rather than collapse. Most importantly, it accustomed millions of viewers to seeing Trump not as a negotiator under pressure, but as a leader issuing commands. The boardroom became rehearsal. The persona became familiar. And familiarity, once established, would later prove politically powerful.

Crafting the Omnipotent Executive Persona

If *The Apprentice* rehabilitated Donald Trump's reputation, it also allowed him to engineer something even more powerful: a carefully constructed executive persona. This was not simply a reflection of who he was. It was a distilled, edited, and amplified version of who he wanted to appear to be—decisive, infallible, and unquestionably in control.

On television, Trump occupied a throne-like seat at the head of the boardroom table. The staging was deliberate. Lighting, camera angles, and editing reinforced hierarchy. Contestants stood before him. Advisors sat beside him but rarely overshadowed him. The structure made clear who held power. Every element from his posture to his cadence projected authority. The audience did not see hesitation. They saw command.

Language played a central role in shaping this persona. Trump spoke in declarative statements. Praise was emphatic. Criticism was blunt. The now-famous phrase "You're fired" was delivered with theatrical certainty, reducing complex business scenarios to a single moment of judgment. The message was simple: leadership means deciding swiftly and visibly. Nuance was edited out. Doubt was invisible.

What makes this persona significant is how it differed from the volatility described by former executives in earlier chapters. On television, unpredictability was recast as strength. Impulsiveness appeared as decisiveness. Ego appeared as confidence. The medium filtered complexity and elevated clarity. By controlling what audiences saw, Trump controlled what they believed about his management style.

The executive persona also reinforced the idea of meritocracy under his authority. Contestants competed fiercely for his approval, suggesting that advancement depended solely on performance. Trump was framed as the ultimate evaluator of talent. This framing subtly expanded his image from businessman to arbiter – someone qualified to judge not just deals, but people.

Over time, repetition cemented this image. Week after week, viewers absorbed the same lesson: Trump is the boss. He assesses, he commands, he eliminates. The performance created familiarity. Familiarity built trust among many viewers. And because television blurs the line between fiction and reality, the persona began to overshadow the historical record.

From a critical standpoint, this construction was strategic brilliance. Trump understood that in the age of mass media, perception could outrun documentation. If audiences saw him as a commanding executive for long enough, the image would carry weight beyond entertainment. Authority performed consistently can feel authentic, even when it is curated.

By the end of this period, Trump was no longer just a real estate developer or brand licensor. He was a cultural figure associated with leadership itself. The executive persona he crafted on television did not stay confined to prime time. It followed him into interviews, speeches, and eventually politics. The boardroom performance became a template. And once authority is performed convincingly enough, the leap from television to national leadership begins to feel less improbable than it should.

Discrepancies Between On-Screen Authority and Off-Screen Management

Television presented Donald Trump as the model of disciplined executive leadership—measured, decisive, and in total command. But when we compare that carefully staged authority with accounts from those who worked with him off camera, a stark contrast appears. The boardroom persona projected clarity and control. The off-screen record reveals volatility, improvisation, and frequent instability.

On *The Apprentice*, decisions appeared swift but reasoned. Contestants were evaluated through structured challenges. Advisors offered input. Trump listened, deliberated briefly, and delivered judgment. The format implied a leader who processed information methodically. Yet former executives from the Trump Organization have described a different reality in business settings. Barbara Res and others have recalled instances of impulsive decision-making, abrupt reversals, and emotionally charged reactions to setbacks. Where the television persona suggested consistency, internal accounts often describe unpredictability.

The difference extended to preparation and depth. On screen, Trump appeared intimately familiar with operational details. Off screen, former associates have noted that he sometimes relied heavily on summaries and instinct rather than granular review. George Ross, who worked closely with Trump for years, acknowledged in interviews that Trump preferred high-level framing and bold negotiation tactics over detailed operational management. That preference did not prevent success, but it contrasts sharply with the image of exhaustive executive oversight portrayed on television.

Even the signature phrase "You're fired" illustrates the gap. On *The Apprentice*, termination was theatrical but clean. Decisions were framed as merit-based and final. In business reality, departures were often more complicated, shaped by legal agreements, renegotiations, or internal friction. Former executives have described environments where loyalty and personal alignment influenced outcomes as much as performance metrics. The simplicity of televised authority masked the complexity and messiness of real-world management.

The editing process itself played a decisive role in shaping perception. Hours of footage were condensed into narrative arcs that reinforced Trump's decisiveness and control. Hesitations, contradictions, or chaotic exchanges rarely made it to air. The result was a version of leadership purified for entertainment, stripped of ambiguity and conflict. What audiences saw was not necessarily false, but it was incomplete.

From a critical perspective, these discrepancies matter because they reveal how authority was manufactured. Television rewarded clarity, dominance, and punchlines. Real management demanded patience, collaboration, and accountability. The former was amplified. The latter was often sidelined. Over time, the public image of Trump as a master executive gained cultural traction, even as former insiders painted a more uneven portrait.

This divergence between performance and practice became one of the most consequential dynamics of Trump's later career. Millions of viewers internalized the televised version of his leadership. Fewer examined the documented accounts from boardrooms and financial crises. The boardroom character was consistent and confident. The historical record was more volatile.

By understanding this discrepancy, we begin to see how media can reshape memory and redefine credibility. Authority, when staged convincingly enough, can overshadow lived experience. And in Trump's case, the persona built under studio lights would eventually carry political weight far beyond the set where it was created.

Reinforcement of Infallibility

When *The Apprentice* reached millions of viewers each week, it did more than rebuild Donald Trump's public reputation. It created a feedback loop of affirmation. Every episode ended the same way: Trump seated at the head of the table, delivering judgment without challenge. The audience saw him win repeatedly. They saw contestants defer to him. They saw success framed as the natural outcome of his instinct. Over time, that repetition did not just influence viewers, it likely reinforced Trump's own perception of infallibility.

Television is not a neutral mirror. It magnifies. The applause lines, the ratings, the media coverage that followed each season—all served as public validation. Trump was no longer defending himself from bankers or restructuring debt under pressure. He was receiving weekly confirmation that his persona resonated. Interviews celebrated him as a symbol of executive strength. Magazine covers elevated him. Viewers repeated his catchphrases. Affirmation became constant.

Psychologically, mass affirmation can alter self-perception. When millions watch you deliver decisive verdicts and respond with approval, doubt becomes harder to access. The on-screen version of Trump—calm, commanding, superior—was rewarded repeatedly. That reward system reinforced the behavior. Confidence hardened. Criticism felt increasingly disconnected from lived experience. If the public embraced the image of mastery, why question it?

Former associates have suggested that Trump was highly responsive to ratings and public attention. Success on television was treated as proof of broader relevance. The line between performance and identity narrowed. The boardroom persona did not remain confined to the studio. It migrated into interviews, speeches, and eventually political rhetoric. The certainty displayed on television became habitual.

Critically, mass affirmation can crowd out corrective feedback. In business, financial failure had imposed limits. In television, there were fewer structural checks. The format guaranteed prominence. Editing minimized contradiction. Advisors on the show reinforced his authority rather than challenging it. The environment insulated him from visible dissent. The audience saw affirmation; Trump experienced it.

This reinforcement matters because it amplified a preexisting trait: resistance to doubt. Earlier chapters have shown how Trump responded to crisis with defensiveness rather than introspection. Television provided the opposite experience – steady validation rather than constraint. Where banks once imposed limits, viewers now imposed applause. The result was a strengthening of conviction that instinct, not deliberation, was sufficient.

By the end of the show's early seasons, Trump was not merely a businessman who survived bankruptcy. He was a cultural figure repeatedly affirmed as decisive and successful. The psychological impact of that sustained validation cannot be separated from what followed. When he later entered politics, he did so while already accustomed to mass attention, accustomed to commanding an audience, and accustomed to equating popularity with correctness.

Infallibility, when reinforced weekly before millions, can begin to feel earned. And once that feeling takes hold, contradiction is no longer just disagreement. Instead, it becomes resistance to a self-image forged under the brightest lights.

Authority Performed, Authority Believed

By the end of this chapter, we see that television did not simply enhance Donald Trump's brand—it redefined it. *The Apprentice* transformed him from a controversial developer with a complicated financial history into a weekly embodiment of executive certainty. The boardroom was scripted, edited, and staged, but the impression it left was powerful and durable. Millions came to associate Trump not with bankruptcy filings or debt restructurings, but with decisive leadership and unchallenged command.

"You're fired — and I'm televised."

The discrepancies between on-screen authority and off-screen management did not weaken the image. They were largely invisible to the audience. What remained visible was repetition: Trump judging, Trump firing, Trump winning. Over time, that repetition reshaped public perception. Authority, when performed consistently enough, begins to feel authentic. And once felt, it becomes politically transferable.

Perhaps most importantly, the show reinforced Trump's own self-conception. Years of mass affirmation strengthened instincts already present—confidence hardened into certainty, confrontation into strength, instinct into virtue. The feedback loop between performance and praise deepened. The persona that had once been cultivated strategically now operated almost seamlessly.

As we move forward, the question shifts from media to ambition. If television provided national familiarity and manufactured authority, what happens when that authority seeks a larger arena? The next stage of Trump's journey moves from boardrooms and studios into politics – not as an outsider experimenting, but as a figure already trained in spectacle, conditioned by affirmation, and convinced of his own indispensability. The rehearsal is complete. The stage is about to change.

PART IV – FROM COMMENTATOR TO POLITICAL ACTOR

Chapter 8: Political Curiosity and Opportunism

By the time Donald Trump began openly engaging with politics, he was no stranger to power, publicity, or confrontation. He had built towers, survived financial crisis, mastered litigation, and reintroduced himself to millions through television. What politics offered was not entirely new terrain, it was a larger stage. But before he became a candidate, he was something else: curious, exploratory, and strategically opportunistic.

Trump's relationship with politics did not begin with a firm ideological foundation. It evolved. Over the years, he shifted party affiliations, flirted with different political identities, and tested public reaction through interviews and exploratory committees. What we see in this chapter is not a steady ideological progression, but a pattern of experimentation. Politics became another arena in which visibility, leverage, and timing mattered.

This chapter examines how Trump positioned himself around issues long before he formally sought office. We trace his shifting affiliations between Democrat, Republican, and Reform Party alignments. We explore how he used political commentary as a tool for relevance, stepping into national debates with bold, often controversial statements that kept his name in circulation. Public policy was frequently framed less as doctrine and more as disruption.

Critically, we must ask: was this evolution conviction-driven, or opportunity-driven? Trump's history suggests that he was attentive to public mood and media opportunity. Political statements often coincided with moments of national attention. The instinct to test boundaries, provoke reaction, and measure response did not begin in campaign rallies—it began years earlier in interviews and talk show appearances.

As we move through this chapter, we explore how political curiosity gradually sharpened into calculation. The instincts honed in business, litigation, and television—dominance, narrative control, and responsiveness to audience reaction—began to merge with national issues. What started as commentary would eventually harden into ambition. And by the time Trump formally entered the political arena, he would do so not as a novice, but as a seasoned performer accustomed to commanding attention and reframing conflict.

The question is not when Trump first thought about politics. The question is how long he had been rehearsing for it.

Trump's Early Political Statements

Long before Donald Trump formally entered a presidential race, he was testing the waters of politics in public. What stands out in these early years is not ideological consistency, but flexibility. Trump did not anchor himself firmly to one party or philosophy. Instead, he moved across political lines, adjusting his language depending on the audience, the moment, and the media opportunity.

In the 1980s, Trump publicly aligned himself with Republican economic themes, particularly around trade and foreign competition. In a 1987 full-page newspaper advertisement published in major outlets such as *The New York Times*, he criticized U.S. foreign policy and argued that allies like Japan were taking advantage of American markets. The message was nationalistic and confrontational. It framed America as exploited and weak in negotiation – an early preview of rhetoric that would later define his campaigns.

Yet during the 1990s and early 2000s, Trump's political identification shifted. He registered as a Democrat in 2001 and publicly praised Democratic figures, including Bill and Hillary Clinton. In interviews, he expressed support for positions that were not traditionally conservative, including more liberal stances on healthcare and social issues at certain points. For example, in a 1999 interview while exploring a Reform Party presidential run, Trump described himself as "very pro-choice" and advocated for universal healthcare coverage—positions that diverged sharply from later Republican orthodoxy.

In 1999 and 2000, Trump briefly pursued the Reform Party nomination, appearing on programs like *Meet the Press* to discuss a potential campaign. During these appearances, he presented himself as an outsider willing to challenge both major parties. His tone emphasized independence rather than loyalty. Policy positions seemed adaptable, but the central message remained consistent: the system was failing, and he alone possessed the strength to fix it.

These shifts reveal more than evolving opinion. They suggest a leader attuned to political opportunity rather than constrained by doctrine. Trump's statements often mirrored populist currents already present in the electorate—trade resentment in the 1980s, anti-establishment frustration in the late 1990s. Instead of building a platform rooted in party identity, he appeared to build one rooted in audience reaction.

Critically, this cross-party positioning insulated him from ideological accountability. Because he did not present himself as a traditional partisan, he could pivot without fully explaining the shift. Supporters often interpreted flexibility as independence. Critics saw inconsistency. But the pattern remained: Trump entered political conversations when they amplified his relevance and adjusted tone when the landscape changed.

By the time he formally rejoined the Republican Party and mounted a serious presidential campaign, these earlier shifts were reframed not as contradictions, but as evidence of deal-making pragmatism. The fluidity across party lines had served its purpose. It kept him visible. It allowed experimentation. And it reinforced a central instinct—politics, like business and media, was an arena where positioning mattered more than allegiance.

Shifting Affiliations and Ideological Inconsistency

If we examine Donald Trump's political trajectory before his presidential campaign, one theme emerges clearly: fluidity. His party registration and public policy positions shifted repeatedly over three decades. These changes were not subtle recalibrations within a stable framework. They were visible moves across ideological lines, often accompanied by rhetoric that contradicted earlier statements.

In the 1980s, Trump publicly aligned himself with Republican themes, particularly around trade and national strength. His 1987 newspaper advertisements criticizing U.S. foreign policy framed America as economically exploited by foreign allies—a message that would later resurface in his 2016 campaign. Yet at that time, Trump had not firmly anchored himself within Republican structures. His political commentary was issue-based and media-driven rather than party-rooted.

By 1999, Trump formally entered politics through the Reform Party, exploring a presidential run. During a televised interview on *Meet the Press*, he described himself as "very pro-choice" and supported a ban on assault weapons. He also spoke favorably about universal healthcare coverage, stating that he believed the government should ensure people receive care. These positions placed him well outside the conservative orthodoxy that would later define his Republican identity.

In 2001, Trump changed his registration to Democrat. Over the next several years, he expressed admiration for Democratic leaders, including Bill Clinton. Public donation records show that he contributed to candidates from both parties. During this period, he praised aspects of Democratic governance in New York and positioned himself as socially moderate. The ideological through-line was difficult to identify beyond a preference for strong leadership and negotiation.

By 2009, Trump had re-registered as a Republican. Around the same time, his rhetoric hardened on issues such as immigration and national identity. The "birther" controversy, which he amplified in 2011 by publicly questioning President Barack Obama's birthplace, marked a turning point. The issue elevated Trump's profile within conservative media circles and aligned him more closely with populist elements inside the Republican base.

Throughout these transitions, Trump rarely framed his shifts as ideological reversals. Instead, he described them as pragmatic adjustments or reflections of changing circumstances. In interviews, he argued that he had been disappointed by both parties at different times. This framing allowed him to cast flexibility as independence rather than inconsistency.

Critically, ideological inconsistency did not appear to undermine his appeal among segments of the electorate. For many supporters, Trump's willingness to move across party lines reinforced the image of a dealmaker unbound by partisan constraints. To critics, however, the pattern suggested opportunism – positions recalibrated to maximize attention and advantage rather than grounded in coherent doctrine.

When we place these shifts in context, a pattern becomes visible. Trump's core themes—strength, negotiation, national leverage, personal authority—remained relatively stable. Specific policy positions, however, moved according to timing and audience. Trade nationalism appeared in the 1980s and reemerged in 2016. Social moderation in the late 1990s gave way to cultural conservatism when that alignment proved electorally advantageous. The constant was not ideology; it was positioning.

This ideological fluidity prepared Trump for a political environment increasingly skeptical of traditional party structures. By the time he launched his presidential campaign, he could credibly claim to be an outsider to both establishments. His prior affiliations allowed him to argue that he had seen the system from multiple angles and rejected it. In this sense, inconsistency became asset rather than liability.

The broader implication is significant. Trump's path into politics was not shaped by long-term ideological evolution. It was shaped by responsiveness to opportunity, media visibility, and shifting public sentiment. Party affiliation was a vehicle, not a destination. And that flexibility would later allow him to reshape the party he ultimately chose to lead.

Recollections of Trump's Limited Interest in Policy Detail

As Donald Trump moved from political curiosity to serious candidacy, a recurring observation emerged from those who briefed and advised him: his engagement with policy detail was often shallow, selective, or secondary to messaging. This pattern did not originate in the White House. It appeared during his early campaign preparation and had echoes in his business career, where broad framing and instinct frequently took precedence over granular analysis.

Sam Nunberg, an early campaign aide in 2015, told reporters that Trump's strength lay in broad themes rather than policy depth. Nunberg recalled that Trump preferred short summaries and strong messaging over extended briefings. According to Nunberg, detailed white papers rarely held his attention; what mattered more was how an issue could be communicated forcefully to voters.

Corey Lewandowski, Trump's first campaign manager, similarly described a candidate who relied heavily on instinct. In interviews and in his book *Let Trump Be Trump*, Lewandowski emphasized that Trump trusted his gut over structured policy preparation. The phrase itself, "let

Trump be Trump" suggested a campaign built around personality and reaction rather than disciplined policy architecture.

Michael Cohen, Trump's longtime personal attorney, has also stated in congressional testimony and memoir that Trump often displayed limited patience for dense policy discussions. Cohen portrayed Trump as someone who gravitated toward headlines and high-level framing, particularly when topics became technical or bureaucratic. While Cohen's later relationship with Trump was adversarial, his recollections align with comments from other advisers who described a preference for brevity and dominance over complexity.

Even Steve Bannon, who joined the campaign in 2016 and later served in the White House, framed Trump less as a policy technician and more as a vessel for populist themes. In interviews, Bannon suggested that Trump's appeal lay in instinctive alignment with voter anger rather than detailed legislative expertise. The emphasis was emotional resonance, not white paper precision.

Journalistic accounts during the campaign also noted moments where Trump appeared unfamiliar with certain policy specifics or contradicted earlier statements. Briefings were often condensed. Policy teams sometimes worked behind the scenes to shape proposals that matched broad directives rather than originating from them. The candidate's focus remained centered on overarching themes: strength, winning, national pride.

Critically, limited interest in policy detail did not prevent political success. In fact, it may have reinforced Trump's outsider persona. Supporters interpreted brevity as authenticity and viewed detailed policy language as establishment jargon. Simplicity became advantage. Complexity became suspicion.

However, from a governance perspective, this pattern raised concerns. Effective policymaking requires sustained engagement with nuance, trade-offs, and institutional limits. When a leader prioritizes instinct and messaging over depth, the risk is that decisions are shaped more by perception than by technical evaluation.

Advisers' recollections do not depict a leader uninterested in power. They depict a leader interested in framing. Trump's engagement often centered on how issues sounded and how they landed with audiences. The details, by many accounts, were secondary.

This dynamic is significant because it bridges business, television, and politics. In each arena, Trump demonstrated a preference for broad strokes and visible dominance over intricate planning. As we move forward in this chapter, that preference becomes central to understanding how he transitioned from commentary to candidacy, not as a policy architect, but as a communicator of grievance and strength.

Politics as Another Arena for Dominance

As Donald Trump moved closer to a formal presidential bid, it became increasingly clear that he did not approach politics as a traditional process of governance. He approached it as competition. The habits formed in business, litigation, and television—win visibly, confront aggressively, never concede weakness—translated seamlessly into political behavior. Policy debates were framed as contests. Opponents were treated as adversaries to be defeated, not colleagues to be persuaded.

In interviews during his exploratory phases, Trump frequently described political leadership in terms drawn from business combat. He emphasized winning, leverage, and strength far more than coalition-building or institutional process. Government was portrayed not as a complex system requiring compromise, but as a failing enterprise needing a stronger chief executive. The language was managerial, even combative. He would "negotiate better deals," "beat China," "crush

ISIS," and "win so much" that Americans would tire of it. The vocabulary signaled dominance, not deliberation.

"Applause is fuel."

This framing extended to how Trump treated critics and media figures. Political disagreement was rarely acknowledged as legitimate ideological difference. It was labeled incompetence, corruption, or hostility. The instinct to escalate, honed through years of legal disputes, became visible in rallies and interviews. He attacked primary opponents personally. He assigned nicknames. He reduced complex debates to sharp, memorable blows. Politics was not a forum for policy nuance. Instead, it was a stage for victory.

Former advisers have observed that Trump's engagement often centered on power dynamics rather than policy frameworks. The question was less "What is the legislative pathway?" and more "Who is strong? Who is weak?" Steve Bannon later suggested that Trump intuitively understood political combat as spectacle, where narrative dominance could outweigh institutional detail. In that environment, governance risked becoming secondary to performance.

Critically, this approach reshaped expectations among supporters. Many voters, frustrated with gridlock and compromise, responded positively to a figure who promised decisive action. Trump's framing turned frustration into energy. The promise was not procedural reform. It was force. Strength would solve what bureaucracy had complicated.

However, governance is structurally different from competition. It requires negotiation across branches of government, respect for institutional limits, and sustained attention to policy detail. Treating politics as another battlefield risks conflating confrontation with effectiveness. In business and television, spectacle could substitute for stability. In governance, the stakes are far broader.

What we see in this period is the merging of persona and ambition. The executive character crafted on television, the combative negotiator refined in courtrooms, the brand-builder obsessed with perception—all converged in politics. The goal was not merely to participate. It was to dominate the narrative space. Governance became framed as a prize to be seized rather than a responsibility to be managed.

This orientation toward dominance would later define not only Trump's campaigns, but his time in office. The instincts were already visible before the first primary vote was cast. Politics was not a new discipline to be learned. It was another arena to be won.

From Experimentation to Intent

By the end of this chapter, a pattern is unmistakable. Donald Trump's path into politics was not anchored in long-held ideological commitment. It was shaped by experimentation, flexibility, and responsiveness to opportunity. Party affiliations shifted. Policy positions evolved. What remained constant was the emphasis on strength, leverage, and visibility. Politics became less about doctrine and more about positioning.

Early statements across party lines allowed Trump to test audiences without being confined by them. Ideological inconsistency did not weaken him; it insulated him. Advisors' recollections reveal a candidate drawn more to message and momentum than to policy architecture. The goal was not to master the intricacies of governance, but to dominate the narrative surrounding it.

As we have seen, Trump approached politics with instincts honed elsewhere. From business he carried confrontation. From litigation he carried escalation. From television he carried performance. Political curiosity gradually transformed into political calculation. Each media appearance, each exploratory committee, each controversial statement functioned as rehearsal.

The key shift now underway is intent. What began as commentary is hardening into ambition. The language grows sharper. The themes grow clearer. Frustration with establishment politics becomes central. The outsider posture solidifies.

In the next chapter, we move from testing the waters to diving in. The stage expands from interviews and exploratory moves to a full campaign. The instincts that were once exploratory become operational. And the question is no longer whether Trump is curious about politics. It is whether politics is ready for the style of combat he brings with him.

Chapter 9: Resentment, Identity, and the Politics of Grievance

By the time Donald Trump formally entered the presidential race, he was no longer experimenting. He was channeling. The themes that had surfaced intermittently for decades—national decline, unfair treatment, betrayal by elites—were no longer scattered remarks. They were central pillars. What had once appeared as personal grievance began to merge with collective frustration.

This chapter examines how Trump transformed resentment into political currency. The rhetoric sharpened. The targets became clearer: political insiders, media institutions, foreign competitors, immigration systems, and cultural elites. Trump did not simply criticize policy outcomes. He framed the system itself as rigged, broken, and hostile to "real" Americans. Identity moved to the foreground.

Resentment, when personalized, is powerful. When collectivized, it becomes combustible. Trump's language consistently drew a line between insiders and outsiders, winners and losers, patriots and exploiters. The grievances he had long expressed in business disputes— being treated unfairly, being obstructed by incompetence—now expanded to encompass the nation itself. America, in his telling, was being taken advantage of, just as he once claimed in trade advertisements decades earlier.

This chapter explores how identity politics and grievance became organizing principles rather than side themes. We examine how resentment was framed not as bitterness, but as clarity. Not as anger, but as awakening. Trump's message resonated with voters who felt overlooked or dislocated. At the same time, it intensified polarization and deepened institutional mistrust.

The politics of grievance is not accidental. It requires amplification, repetition, and emotional precision. Trump understood how to identify wounds whether economic, cultural, or symbolic, and speak directly to them. In doing so, he shifted political discourse away from policy detail and toward emotional allegiance.

As we move through this chapter, we will see how resentment became mobilization, how identity became alignment, and how grievance became strategy. Because once politics is framed as a battle for dignity against betrayal, compromise becomes weakness—and confrontation becomes destiny.

Trump's Rhetoric around Elites, Media, and Institutions

As Donald Trump moved from candidate to political force, one theme became central to his message: the system was corrupt, and the elites who ran it were untrustworthy. This was not an occasional criticism. It was a sustained narrative. Trump framed himself as an outsider battling entrenched interests—politicians, media organizations, corporate leaders, and bureaucratic institutions—that, in his telling, had betrayed ordinary Americans.

His rhetoric toward political elites was blunt and personal. Career politicians were described as weak, incompetent, or corrupt. Washington was portrayed not as a flawed system in need of reform, but as a self-serving machine indifferent to the public. Trump often insisted that he alone could negotiate effectively because he was not beholden to donors or party structures. The implication was powerful: institutions were compromised, and only someone outside them could act decisively.

The media became an even more visible target. Trump did not treat journalists as neutral observers or critics to be rebutted. He framed them as adversaries. During campaign rallies, he pointed physically to press sections and accused reporters of dishonesty. The phrase "fake news" entered his vocabulary and quickly became a defining feature of his political brand. Critical coverage was not framed as disagreement; it was framed as deception. The press, once merely inconvenient in business disputes, became a central antagonist in political storytelling.

Institutions broadly defined—courts, intelligence agencies, regulatory bodies—were also drawn into this rhetoric when they appeared to challenge him. Oversight was portrayed as obstruction. Investigations were labeled witch hunts. Bureaucratic resistance was described as sabotage. In this framework, institutional constraint was not a necessary feature of democratic governance; it was evidence of a rigged system.

What made this rhetoric effective was its emotional precision. Many voters already harbored skepticism toward elites and media. Trump did not invent that distrust. He amplified it. By speaking in absolutes of "the system is broken," and "the media is corrupt", he simplified complex institutional dynamics into moral battles. The language was accessible, memorable, and confrontational.

Critically, this approach also insulated him. If media coverage was negative, it reinforced the narrative of bias. If institutions resisted his actions, it confirmed their corruption. The rhetoric created a self-sealing logic. Any challenge became proof of hostility. Accountability mechanisms were reframed as partisan attack.

The political consequence of this strategy was profound. Trust in institutions weakened further. Polarization intensified. Supporters saw Trump as a fighter against entrenched power. Critics saw him as undermining democratic norms. But the dynamic remained consistent: elites were adversaries, media was suspect, and institutions were obstacles to be overcome.

In turning elites and institutions into rhetorical enemies, Trump did more than energize a base. He reoriented political discourse toward confrontation. Governance became secondary to combat. And once institutions are framed as illegitimate, resisting them no longer appears disruptive, it appears righteous.

Personal Slights Transformed into Political Narratives

One of the most revealing features of Donald Trump's political style is how frequently personal grievances became public themes. What might have remained private resentment was often reframed as national injustice. The line between personal slight and political principle blurred. Criticism was not simply rebutted—it was elevated into proof of systemic bias.

Throughout his business and media career, Trump had demonstrated acute sensitivity to criticism. Negative coverage prompted direct calls to reporters. Critical biographies triggered threats of legal action. This instinct did not fade in politics; it expanded. When questioned about policy competence, Trump reframed the inquiry as establishment hostility toward outsiders. When fact-checkers challenged statements, he cast them as part of a dishonest media apparatus. Personal pushback became evidence of institutional conspiracy.

The pattern intensified during his presidential campaign. Mockery from political rivals was met with counterattack, but the counterattack rarely remained confined to the original exchange. A dispute over crowd size became a broader accusation of media dishonesty. A challenge to his business record became an indictment of elite hypocrisy. What began as a narrow disagreement evolved into a sweeping narrative about corruption and unfair treatment.

Even moments that might have been dismissed as routine political friction were reframed dramatically. When debate moderators pressed him, they were accused of bias. When party leaders withheld early endorsement, they were described as weak or compromised. The response consistently followed the same structure: a personal setback was elevated into a symbolic example of how the system mistreats truth-tellers.

This transformation served a strategic function. By recasting personal slights as collective grievance, Trump fused his own experience with that of his supporters. If he was treated unfairly by elites or media, so too were they. His battles became their battles. The narrative shifted from "Trump versus critics" to "us versus a rigged establishment." Personal sensitivity evolved into populist solidarity.

Critically, this approach discouraged introspection. If every challenge originates from bad faith, then self-examination becomes unnecessary. The rhetorical move from individual dispute to systemic accusation shields the leader from accountability. It also escalates conflict, because the stakes are no longer individual—they are existential.

Over time, this habit of transforming slights into narratives hardened into political identity. Trump did not merely argue policy differences. He cast himself as perpetually targeted, unfairly attacked, and unjustly obstructed. The sense of grievance, once personal and episodic, became continuous and collective.

This pattern matters because it reshapes how leadership responds to opposition. When disagreement is interpreted as persecution, compromise appears as surrender. When criticism is framed as conspiracy, institutions lose legitimacy. The transformation of personal slights into political narratives did more than energize rallies. It redefined conflict as proof of righteousness and that redefinition would shape both campaign and governance alike.

How Longstanding Grievances Found Political Utility

Long before Donald Trump launched a presidential campaign, he had cultivated a worldview shaped by grievance. In business, setbacks were attributed to unfair regulators, hostile lenders, dishonest contractors, or biased journalists. In media disputes, criticism was framed as envy or bad faith. Over decades, this reflex hardened into instinct. When he entered politics, that instinct did not disappear, it expanded. Personal grievance became political instrument.

What had once been disputes over contracts or coverage were repackaged as national struggles. Trump's long-standing complaints about foreign trade partners "taking advantage" of America echoed the language he had used in his 1987 newspaper ads. His suspicion of media institutions, sharpened by years of critical reporting, became a central campaign theme. Even his resentment toward bureaucratic obstacles in development projects resurfaced in attacks on "red tape" and government incompetence. The grievances were not new. The audience was.

This transformation worked because the emotional core of grievance is transferable. Feelings of being blocked, dismissed, or treated unfairly resonate beyond individual circumstance. Trump tapped into economic anxiety, cultural displacement, and distrust of elites—sentiments already present in parts of the electorate. By aligning his personal sense of unfairness with broader voter frustration, he created a shared narrative. If he had been wronged by elites, so had the country.

The utility of grievance lies in its simplicity. It reduces complex problems to identifiable antagonists. Trade deficits become the fault of weak negotiators. Economic stagnation becomes the fault of corrupt politicians. Media criticism becomes the fault of dishonest journalists. The narrative clarifies enemies and elevates the leader as the one willing to fight them. Trump's long-standing habit of naming adversaries translated seamlessly into campaign rhetoric.

Importantly, grievance also fuels loyalty. Supporters who see their frustrations mirrored in a candidate's language feel recognized. Trump's rallies became spaces where resentment was not suppressed but validated. Each criticism from opponents reinforced the storyline of persecution. Each controversy extended the narrative of resistance. The pattern he had practiced for years—turning opposition into affirmation—scaled nationally.

From a critical standpoint, the political utility of grievance carries consequences. When grievance becomes central to identity, governance risks becoming reactive rather than constructive. Policies may be shaped less by strategic planning and more by symbolic retaliation. Institutions are treated not as partners but as adversaries. The energy that mobilizes voters can also entrench division.

For Trump, longstanding grievances were not liabilities. They were assets waiting for amplification. The frustrations that once animated business disputes and media feuds became the emotional backbone of a national campaign. What had been personal became political. What had been episodic became continuous. And in that transformation, grievance shifted from private reflex to governing philosophy.

Former Aides' Accounts of Obsession with Perceived Disrespect

One of the most consistent themes in accounts from former aides is Donald Trump's acute sensitivity to perceived disrespect. Across campaign, transition, and presidency, several advisers have described a leader who measured loyalty and legitimacy not only through policy alignment, but through tone, posture, and personal deference. Criticism was not merely disagreement. It was disrespect. And disrespect demanded response.

Corey Lewandowski, Trump's first campaign manager, wrote in *Let Trump Be Trump* that Trump reacted strongly when he believed he was being slighted. Lewandowski framed this trait as a strength—evidence of toughness—but acknowledged that Trump took public criticism personally and felt compelled to counterpunch. The instinct was not to ignore insult, but to answer it immediately and forcefully.

Michael Cohen, Trump's longtime personal attorney, described a similar pattern in congressional testimony and in his memoir. Cohen stated that Trump often focused intensely on negative press coverage and would demand to know who was responsible. According to Cohen, Trump's first question after critical stories was frequently, "Who said that?" The emphasis was not only on correcting the record, but on identifying the perceived offender. Cohen portrayed a leader who interpreted unfavorable coverage as personal betrayal rather than professional scrutiny.

John Kelly, Trump's former Chief of Staff, reportedly told colleagues that Trump was highly reactive to slights, especially those delivered publicly. According to reporting in outlets such as *The New York Times* and *The Atlantic*, aides spent considerable time managing his responses to media commentary and social media posts that questioned his authority. Rather than dismissing criticism as routine political friction, Trump often elevated it into confrontation.

Even Steve Bannon, who aligned closely with Trump's combative style, acknowledged in interviews that Trump's political strength lay in counterattack. Bannon suggested that Trump thrived when battling critics, turning disputes into proof of authenticity. But embedded in that framing was a recognition: Trump's attention frequently centered on who had challenged him, not simply on what had been argued.

The consequences of this sensitivity were operational as well as rhetorical. Aides have described environments where staff members were cautious in delivering unwelcome news, aware that critical framing might be interpreted as disloyalty. The dynamic echoed earlier business accounts—information was filtered not only for accuracy, but for tone. Maintaining proximity to power required attentiveness to ego.

Critically, obsession with perceived disrespect reshapes leadership priorities. Energy that might be directed toward policy detail can instead be consumed by personal counteroffensives. Social media became a particularly visible outlet for this instinct, with responses often issued swiftly after perceived slights. The cycle reinforced itself: criticism prompted reaction; reaction generated further criticism; further criticism confirmed the sense of hostility.

From a psychological perspective, this pattern connects directly to earlier chapters. Years of legal combat, media battles, and personal branding had conditioned Trump to equate criticism with threat. In politics, that conditioning intensified. Public life guaranteed scrutiny. Scrutiny triggered response. And response became performance.

Former aides' accounts do not describe a leader indifferent to image. They describe one preoccupied with it. Respect was not abstract—it was personal, immediate, and enforceable. In a political environment where dissent is inevitable, such sensitivity ensured that conflict would be constant. And as grievance became political strategy, perceived disrespect became fuel.

Grievance as Governing Energy

By the end of this chapter, it becomes clear that resentment was not a campaign accessory for Donald Trump; it was an engine. Longstanding personal grievances, sharpened over decades in business and media conflict, found political expression at scale. Elites were cast as corrupt. The press was framed as dishonest. Institutions were portrayed as hostile. And personal slights were elevated into proof of systemic betrayal.

What distinguished this approach was not merely its confrontational tone, but its emotional precision. Trump did not invent frustration among voters; he identified it, mirrored it, and personalized it. His own narrative of being obstructed, misrepresented, or treated unfairly fused with broader anxieties about economic displacement, cultural change, and institutional mistrust. In that fusion, grievance became solidarity.

'They started it.'

Former aides' recollections reinforce how deeply personal sensitivity shaped this strategy. Perceived disrespect triggered escalation. Criticism demanded counterattack. Over time, this reflex was no longer episodic, it became continuous. The result was a political style built not around consensus or persuasion, but around resistance and dominance.

The political utility of grievance is powerful. It mobilizes. It clarifies enemies. It transforms complex policy debates into moral struggle. But it also narrows space for compromise and deepens polarization. When leadership defines itself through conflict, every challenge becomes existential. Every disagreement becomes betrayal.

As we move into the next chapter, the energy of grievance evolves into organization. Resentment that once fueled rhetoric now fuels movement. Campaign infrastructure, digital amplification, and rally culture transform emotion into momentum. The question shifts from why grievance resonates to how it mobilizes power. Because once grievance becomes identity, it no longer simply motivates – it commands.

PART V – THE MAKING OF A CONTENDER

Chapter 10: The 2016 Campaign as Personal Validation

When Donald Trump descended the escalator in June 2015 to announce his candidacy for president, the moment was staged like a product launch. The setting was familiar—Trump Tower, the gold surfaces, the branded backdrop. But this was not just a political declaration. It was a culmination. Decades of business battles, media cultivation, ideological repositioning, and grievance politics converged in that announcement. The campaign was not merely about public office. It was about personal vindication.

For years, Trump had sought recognition beyond the skyline. Television had granted him authority in living rooms. Branding had expanded his name globally. But politics offered something deeper: ultimate validation. To win the presidency would not only silence critics, it would elevate him above them. The businessman once questioned for bankruptcies would become commander in chief. The television host once dismissed as entertainer would become head of state. The narrative arc would be complete.

This chapter examines the 2016 campaign not just as a political event, but as a psychological milestone. Trump's rhetoric during the race consistently blurred the line between national restoration and personal triumph. "Make America Great Again" operated on two levels – country and candidate. The restoration of national pride mirrored the restoration of his own authority. Victory would prove not only policy correctness, but personal superiority.

We explore how rallies became arenas of affirmation, how attacks from opponents reinforced the outsider narrative, and how media saturation amplified both criticism and support. The campaign unfolded as a contest, but also as a test. Could the persona built in business and perfected on television withstand the scrutiny of national politics? Could grievance be converted into governance? Could dominance translate into votes?

The 2016 race was about many things – economic anxiety, populist anger, and partisan realignment. But for Trump, it was also something intimate. It was an opportunity to transform decades of confrontation into triumph. The presidency was not simply the next step. It was the ultimate stage. And on that stage, validation awaited.

Campaign Strategy Rooted in Attention Capture

From the earliest days of the 2016 campaign, it became clear that Donald Trump was not running a conventional operation built around incremental coalition-building. Traditional presidential campaigns focus heavily on expanding alliances, courting party leaders, consolidating demographic blocs, and constructing broad consensus platforms. Trump's approach was different. His strategy prioritized attention above all else.

Rather than carefully calibrate messaging to avoid controversy, Trump leaned into statements that guaranteed media saturation. His announcement speech, particularly the remarks about immigration, generated immediate national coverage—much of it critical. Yet the controversy ensured that his candidacy dominated headlines. Where other candidates struggled for airtime, Trump commanded it. The campaign quickly demonstrated a pattern: provocation produced attention; attention produced momentum.

Data from the primary season reflected this imbalance. Trump received an unprecedented volume of free media coverage compared to his Republican rivals. Cable networks aired his rallies live. Interviews were frequent. Social media amplified every statement. While competitors invested heavily in ground operations and donor networks, Trump capitalized on constant visibility. The spectacle became the engine.

Coalition-building within the Republican establishment was secondary. Trump openly challenged party leadership, criticized primary opponents by name, and rejected policy orthodoxy on issues such as trade and foreign intervention. Instead of smoothing divisions, he exploited them. The campaign's energy centered less on unifying factions and more on dominating the conversation. Loyalty was built through shared grievance and spectacle, not negotiated compromise.

This approach extended to digital strategy. Trump's use of Twitter bypassed traditional party intermediaries. He communicated directly with supporters, often in sharp, declarative bursts. Each tweet could reset the news cycle. The strategy did not require broad policy agreement. It required engagement. Attention whether positive or negative kept the campaign at the center of public discourse.

Critically, attention capture proved electorally effective in a crowded primary field. With multiple candidates dividing establishment support, Trump's constant visibility consolidated a passionate base. He did not need to win every demographic. He needed to dominate narrative space. The Republican primary became less a policy seminar and more a media competition, and Trump excelled in that arena.

From a critical perspective, this strategy reshaped modern campaigning. It demonstrated that saturation can substitute for organization, and spectacle can overshadow structure. Coalition-building traditionally relies on negotiation and ideological alignment. Attention capture relies on disruption and amplification. Trump chose the latter—and it carried him through the primaries and into the general election.

The implications are significant. When attention becomes the primary currency of politics, policy detail recedes. Outrage and loyalty become mobilizing tools. Governance risks becoming an extension of campaign performance. But in 2016, the objective was not governance, it was victory. And in that contest, commanding the spotlight proved more decisive than assembling consensus.

Emotional Resonance over Policy Coherence

If we look closely at the 2016 campaign, one feature stands out immediately: emotional intensity consistently outweighed policy precision. Donald Trump's rallies were not structured around detailed legislative frameworks or white papers. They were structured around themes—anger, pride, betrayal, restoration. The language was simple, repetitive, and emotionally charged. And it worked.

Rather than present lengthy policy proposals, Trump relied on slogans that condensed complex issues into visceral promises. "Build the wall." "Drain the swamp." "Make America Great Again." Each phrase carried emotional weight. They suggested action, clarity, and moral contrast. The details of funding mechanisms, legislative pathways, or diplomatic consequences were secondary. What mattered was how the promise felt.

Immigration policy offers a clear example. Trump's rhetoric framed immigration not primarily as a bureaucratic or economic challenge, but as a threat to safety and sovereignty. The emotional appeal of security, control, and national identity preceded technical discussion. Similarly, on trade, he did not focus heavily on tariff structures or multilateral frameworks. He emphasized unfairness, exploitation, and winning. The argument was intuitive rather than procedural.

Even when policy positions shifted or lacked internal consistency, the emotional through-line remained steady. Supporters were less drawn to detailed coherence than to conviction. Trump projected certainty. He spoke in absolutes. He rejected hedging language. For voters frustrated with political ambiguity, that clarity felt refreshing, even if the specifics were fluid.

Former campaign aides have acknowledged that Trump often preferred broad framing to policy depth. The strategy was deliberate. Detailed explanations risked dilution of message. Emotional resonance kept the audience engaged. Rally speeches frequently returned to stories of loss—lost jobs, lost respect, lost control. The narrative was less about legislative mechanics and more about restoration of dignity.

Critically, emotional politics creates loyalty that policy debate alone cannot. When voters feel seen and validated, technical inconsistencies carry less weight. Trump's campaign did not ask supporters to memorize position papers. It asked them to feel wronged and to feel powerful in response. That emotional transaction built cohesion.

From a strategic standpoint, this approach also neutralized traditional fact-checking dynamics. When rhetoric operates at the level of feeling, data alone cannot dislodge it. Critics who pointed out contradictions or feasibility challenges often appeared pedantic compared to the emotional clarity of the message. The campaign became a contest of narrative intensity rather than policy architecture.

However, the reliance on emotional resonance carried implications. It deepened polarization, simplified complex problems, and reduced space for nuanced compromise. The emotional appeal mobilized turnout but left governance questions unresolved. Policy coherence is tested in office; emotional resonance is tested at the ballot box.

In 2016, the ballot box was the immediate goal. Trump's campaign demonstrated that in a media-saturated environment, emotional clarity can eclipse policy complexity. The message did not need to be internally seamless. It needed to be emotionally compelling. And for millions of voters, it was.

Insiders' Descriptions of Chaos, Impulsiveness, and Loyalty Tests

While the public face of the 2016 campaign often appeared unified and energetic, insiders have described a very different internal environment—one marked by volatility, abrupt decision-making, and constant tests of loyalty. As in earlier chapters of Trump's career, the pattern of centralized authority and reactive leadership resurfaced under the pressure of a national race.

Corey Lewandowski, Trump's first campaign manager, later wrote that the campaign operated with minimal traditional structure in its early months. Decisions were often made quickly, sometimes without consultation with senior staff. Lewandowski framed this as agility, but others described it as improvisation bordering on chaos. Rapid shifts in messaging, staffing changes, and last-minute strategy adjustments became common.

Sam Nunberg, an early aide, told reporters after his dismissal that the campaign environment could be erratic. He suggested that proximity to Trump depended less on policy expertise than on personal alignment. Staff who challenged direction risked marginalization. The pattern echoed accounts from Trump's business years: dissent was often interpreted as disloyalty.

Later campaign figures offered similar reflections. Michael Cohen described a culture in which loyalty to Trump personally outweighed adherence to institutional norms. Public defense of Trump, even amid controversy, was treated as proof of commitment. Those who hesitated or sought nuance could find themselves sidelined. Loyalty was not abstract; it was demonstrated publicly and repeatedly.

Journalistic investigations during and after the campaign documented frequent turnover among senior staff. Lewandowski was removed in mid-2016. Paul Manafort, who replaced him, resigned amid controversy. Steve Bannon and Kellyanne Conway brought different strategic approaches, often operating within an atmosphere of internal rivalry. Multiple aides later acknowledged that decision-making could pivot suddenly based on Trump's mood, media coverage, or rally reaction.

Impulsiveness also characterized public communication. Tweets were sometimes issued without coordination with communications staff. Policy statements delivered at rallies occasionally diverged from prepared remarks. Advisors often found themselves adjusting strategy in response to remarks that had already been broadcast nationally. The pace was relentless, and control was centralized.

Critically, the internal culture reflected the same themes visible externally. Authority flowed from Trump personally. Stability depended on alignment. Staff operated in an environment where public loyalty was a form of currency. This dynamic created intensity and cohesion among core supporters, but it also generated unpredictability.

From a broader perspective, the campaign's internal volatility reinforced Trump's outsider image. The absence of polished structure contrasted sharply with conventional political operations. Supporters saw authenticity where critics saw disorder. The very chaos described by insiders became, for many voters, evidence that Trump was not part of the establishment machine.

Yet the pattern raised important questions. Campaigns are rehearsal for governance. If impulsiveness and loyalty tests defined internal culture during the race, what would they mean in office? The tension between energy and stability, between instinct and structure, would not disappear with victory. It would follow him into the next chapter, where the stakes would be far greater than campaign optics.

Media Amplification Feeding Behavioral Escalation

One of the most powerful feedback loops of the 2016 campaign was the relationship between Donald Trump's rhetoric and the media environment surrounding it. The more provocative the statement, the more coverage it generated. The more coverage it generated, the greater the incentive to repeat the pattern. Attention did not merely follow behavior, it reinforced it.

From the outset, Trump demonstrated an instinct for dominating news cycles. A controversial remark about immigration, a sharp insult directed at a rival, or an unexpected policy declaration would trigger hours—sometimes days—of continuous coverage across cable networks and digital platforms. Critics condemned the statements. Supporters defended them. Either way, Trump remained at the center of the conversation.

"Instant policy."

Data analyses conducted after the primaries showed that Trump received dramatically more "earned media" than his opponents. Cable networks aired rallies live, sometimes in full. Interviews were frequent and often extended. Social media platforms amplified clips within minutes. The campaign did not need to spend proportionally to remain visible. The ecosystem itself supplied oxygen.

This amplification shaped behavior. When escalation produced coverage, escalation became rational. Measured comments rarely dominated headlines. Confrontational ones did. The incentive structure rewarded sharpness over subtlety. Each time controversy drove ratings, the dynamic deepened. Media organizations, chasing viewership, aired more. Trump, observing the attention, pushed further.

The feedback loop blurred the line between strategy and instinct. Impulsive tweets or rally remarks were not always filtered through traditional communications discipline. Yet when those moments generated saturation coverage, they functioned as strategic assets. Even negative coverage reinforced Trump's outsider narrative, validating claims that the media was obsessed, biased, or hostile.

Critically, amplification also normalized escalation. Language that might once have been politically disqualifying became part of a continuous cycle. Outrage fatigue set in. What shocked one week became routine the next. Boundaries shifted incrementally. The political discourse hardened.

Former campaign insiders have acknowledged that media response influenced tone and timing. When certain themes resonated strongly— crowd reactions, cable coverage spikes—those themes were repeated. Rally rhetoric was calibrated not solely around policy impact but around emotional response and airtime.

The broader consequence of this loop was acceleration. Behavior escalated because amplification rewarded it. Amplification intensified because behavior escalated. The cycle became self-sustaining. Trump's campaign did not merely adapt to the modern media environment – it exploited and reshaped it.

By the time the general election approached, the dynamic was entrenched. Media coverage had become both adversary and amplifier. Criticism energized the base. Controversy ensured dominance of narrative space. Escalation was no longer episodic; it was structural.

This phenomenon is central to understanding the 2016 campaign. Attention was not incidental—it was fuel. And once a campaign learns that outrage guarantees oxygen, restraint becomes strategically irrational. The escalation was not accidental. It was reinforced, rewarded, and repeated.

Validation Through Victory

By the end of the 2016 campaign, one truth was undeniable: Donald Trump had transformed attention into triumph. What began as a candidacy dismissed by many as spectacle evolved into a political movement fueled by emotional resonance, media dominance, and relentless escalation. Coalition-building had been secondary. Policy coherence had often taken a back seat to intensity. Yet the strategy worked.

The campaign operated less as a conventional policy operation and more as a vehicle for personal validation. Each rally affirmed loyalty. Each controversy amplified presence. Each attack from opponents reinforced the outsider narrative. Media amplification fed escalation, and escalation guaranteed coverage. The cycle, once established, became unstoppable.

Internally, insiders described chaos and loyalty tests. Externally, supporters saw authenticity and strength. The difference between disorder and disruption depended largely on perspective. What critics interpreted as impulsiveness, many voters interpreted as candor. What establishment figures labeled recklessness, supporters framed as refusal to bow.

Most critically, the campaign completed a long arc. The businessman once doubted by lenders, the television personality once dismissed as entertainer, the outsider long critical of elites – each identity converged. Winning the presidency did more than secure office. It validated a worldview: that dominance works, that grievance mobilizes, and that attention can overpower structure.

But validation carries consequence. A campaign built on escalation must now govern. A movement rooted in grievance must now translate anger into policy. The next chapter moves beyond the victory celebration and into the test of governance. Because the presidency is not a rally stage. It is an institution. And institutions respond differently to confrontation than crowds do.

Chapter 11: Dominating the Party

Winning the presidency was only one battle. The next contest was internal. Once in office, Donald Trump faced not only opposition from Democrats and the media, but also skepticism within his own party. Many Republican leaders had resisted his candidacy during the primaries. Some questioned his ideological consistency. Others doubted his discipline. But victory altered the equation. Power reshapes loyalty.

This chapter examines how Trump moved from being an insurgent candidate to the central force within the Republican Party. The same instincts that defined his campaign—dominance, confrontation, personal loyalty—now operated inside party structures. Endorsements became currency. Criticism became risk. Over time, the balance shifted. Where party leaders once hesitated, many recalibrated.

Trump's relationship with Republican institutions was complex from the outset. He did not rise through traditional party ranks. He did not rely heavily on long-standing policy networks. Instead, he relied on direct connection to voters and media visibility. That connection gave him leverage. Elected officials understood that crossing him could carry electoral consequences, especially in primary contests.

We will explore how public criticism of Trump from Republican figures often prompted swift retaliation via social media, public statements, or endorsement of challengers. Loyalty became visible and measurable. Silence was sometimes treated as dissent. The party, which had once shaped its candidates, increasingly adjusted itself to the preferences of its president.

The chapter also considers the psychological dimension. For Trump, dominating the party was not simply strategic. It was consistent with his broader approach to authority. Coalition within the party was less about shared ideology and more about alignment with him personally. The line between party loyalty and personal loyalty blurred.

As we move through this chapter, we will see how Trump consolidated influence, reshaped party messaging, and redefined internal dissent. The outsider who had challenged the establishment now became its central force. And in doing so, he demonstrated that political power, once secured, can be leveraged not only against opponents, but within one's own ranks.

Trump's Relationship with the Republican Establishment

From the beginning of his 2016 campaign, Donald Trump's relationship with the Republican establishment was tense, transactional, and deeply distrustful. Party leaders, major donors, and long-serving lawmakers initially viewed him as an unpredictable outsider who threatened ideological coherence and electoral stability. Trump, in turn, portrayed them as weak, ineffective, and disconnected from the party's grassroots voters. The conflict was not accidental. It was foundational.

During the Republican primaries, Trump openly attacked high-profile figures within his own party. He criticized former President George W. Bush's foreign policy decisions. He mocked Senator John McCain's war record. He dismissed rivals such as Jeb Bush and Marco Rubio with personal nicknames that dominated headlines. These attacks were not merely campaign tactics—they were signals. Trump was not seeking the establishment's approval. He was challenging its authority.

Many Republican leaders hesitated to endorse him even after he secured the nomination. Some distanced themselves publicly. Others offered reluctant support. Yet once Trump won the presidency, the dynamic shifted dramatically. Electoral reality forced recalibration. The base that had propelled Trump to victory was now central to Republican electoral strategy. Lawmakers who opposed him risked alienating primary voters energized by his style and rhetoric.

Trump capitalized on this leverage. His endorsement became a powerful instrument within the party. Public praise elevated allies; public criticism invited primary challenges. Through rallies, social media, and direct messaging, he maintained a direct channel to Republican voters— often bypassing institutional intermediaries. This direct connection altered the traditional hierarchy. Influence flowed not solely through party committees, but through Trump's personal platform.

The establishment faced a dilemma. Aligning with Trump ensured access to his base and preserved electoral viability. Opposing him risked marginalization. Over time, many party figures adjusted their positions to mirror his priorities, particularly on immigration, trade nationalism, and confrontational media rhetoric. The party's policy language began to reflect his themes.

Yet the relationship remained transactional. Trump valued loyalty visibly and publicly. Support was expected, especially during controversies. Those who voiced dissent, whether on foreign policy, impeachment, or rhetoric, often faced direct criticism. The pattern mirrored earlier chapters of his career: loyalty strengthened proximity; dissent risked exclusion.

From a broader perspective, Trump's relationship with the Republican establishment illustrates a reversal of traditional political dynamics. Instead of the party shaping the candidate, the candidate reshaped the party. Institutional norms bent toward the energy of his base. Ideological coherence adjusted to accommodate his message. The outsider, once resisted, became the center of gravity.

Critically, this shift did not eliminate internal tension. It suppressed it. Differences over strategy and tone persisted beneath the surface. But the electoral power of Trump's movement limited open resistance. The establishment adapted because it calculated that survival required adaptation.

In the end, Trump's relationship with the Republican establishment was not about reconciliation—it was about realignment. The party did not absorb him. He absorbed it. And in doing so, he demonstrated that modern political authority can derive less from institutional endorsement and more from personal dominance over a mobilized base.

Use of Public Shaming to Secure Compliance

As Donald Trump consolidated influence within the Republican Party, one of his most consistent tools was public pressure. Where traditional party leaders relied on private negotiation and backroom persuasion, Trump frequently chose visible confrontation. Public shaming—often delivered through rallies, interviews, or social media— became a mechanism for enforcing loyalty and discouraging dissent.

The pattern was direct. Republican officials who criticized Trump or hesitated to support key initiatives often found themselves singled out publicly. Tweets questioned their competence, loyalty, or electoral strength. At rallies, names were mentioned, sometimes followed by boos from the crowd. The message to both the target and the broader party was unmistakable: deviation would be noticed and punished.

This tactic was particularly effective in an era of hyper-partisan primaries. Trump's endorsement carried significant weight with Republican voters. Conversely, his opposition could invite well-funded primary challengers. Lawmakers understood the risk. Several high-profile Republicans who criticized Trump during or after his presidency faced intense primary battles fueled by pro-Trump candidates. Even when those challengers did not succeed, the signal was clear—public dissent had electoral cost.

The shaming extended beyond elected officials. Party operatives, commentators, and even former administration officials were labeled disloyal when they broke ranks. Nicknames and sharp descriptors, once reserved for Democratic opponents during the campaign, were now applied within the party. The tactic blurred the line between intra-party disagreement and outright betrayal.

Critically, the use of public shaming functioned as both punishment and deterrent. Those targeted experienced immediate reputational strain within the party base. Those observing adjusted behavior accordingly. Silence became safer than critique. Alignment became visible and performative.

From a strategic standpoint, this approach centralized authority. Instead of relying on institutional hierarchy, Trump leveraged direct communication with voters. The public became an enforcement mechanism. Compliance was secured not solely through policy agreement, but through fear of public rebuke and primary challenge.

However, this dynamic carried consequences. Public shaming reduces space for internal deliberation. Lawmakers become cautious in offering independent judgment. Policy debates narrow. When loyalty to a figure outweighs loyalty to institutional process, governance becomes personalized.

The tactic was consistent with Trump's broader operating style, evident in business and campaign chapters alike. Confront critics publicly. Escalate rather than negotiate quietly. Transform disagreement into spectacle. Within the Republican Party, the effect was profound. Compliance was not always enthusiastic, but it was visible.

By turning public platforms into tools of discipline, Trump redefined party leadership as personal dominance. Support was measured not only by votes, but by vocal affirmation. And once that standard took hold, dissent within the party required not just disagreement but courage.

Transformation of Party Norms around Leadership and Dissent

As Donald Trump tightened his hold on the Republican Party, the transformation was not merely electoral, it was cultural. Party norms that had long governed leadership behavior, internal disagreement, and public messaging began to shift. What had once been managed quietly through committee structures and private negotiation increasingly played out in public and personal terms.

Traditionally, party leadership functioned through layered authority. Senior lawmakers shaped legislative priorities. Committee chairs negotiated compromises. Dissent, while present, was often expressed behind closed doors. Under Trump's influence, this architecture changed. Authority flowed less from institutional seniority and more from alignment with him personally. Proximity to Trump and the willingness to defend him publicly became markers of influence.

One of the most notable shifts concerned dissent. In previous eras, disagreement within the party was considered part of healthy internal debate. Under Trump, dissent risked being labeled disloyalty. Public criticism of the president was often met with swift rebuttal, sometimes amplified by Trump's own social media presence. Lawmakers who voted against his priorities or voiced skepticism frequently faced primary challengers supported by Trump or his allies.

This transformation was visible during major flashpoints, including impeachment proceedings and certification of election results. Republican officials who broke ranks were subjected to intense pressure from segments of the party base. In some cases, state party organizations formally censured members who had voted to impeach Trump. The message signaled a recalibration of norms: loyalty to the leader was increasingly prioritized over institutional independence.

The rhetorical style of party leadership also shifted. Confrontation became more acceptable, even expected. Language that once might have been considered politically risky became normalized. Media skepticism hardened into open hostility. The party's public identity began to reflect Trump's combative tone and populist framing, particularly on issues of immigration, trade, and cultural grievance.

Critically, this transformation extended beyond rhetoric to structural incentives. Primary elections grew more central to party discipline. Fear of being "primaried" by a pro-Trump challenger discouraged open dissent. Campaign endorsements became instruments of enforcement. The base, energized by Trump's direct communication, played a larger role in shaping candidate viability.

Supporters argued that these changes democratized the party, making it more responsive to grassroots voters. Critics contended that the shift weakened deliberative norms and reduced space for internal diversity. Both interpretations acknowledge the same reality: the party's center of gravity moved.

Leadership, under Trump's influence, became more personalized. Authority was not merely derived from office. Instead, it was reinforced through public affirmation and visible loyalty. Dissent was not simply disagreement—it was potential betrayal. The boundaries of acceptable critique narrowed.

This transformation reshaped the Republican Party's identity and internal dynamics. The establishment that once hesitated to embrace Trump found itself operating within a framework he had redefined. The norms of leadership and dissent adjusted accordingly. And once norms change, they rarely revert easily. The question moving forward is not whether the party changed, but how durable those changes will prove to be in the long arc of American politics.

Accounts of Trump Equating Loyalty with Personal Allegiance

One of the most consistent observations from former advisers is that Donald Trump defined loyalty in deeply personal terms. In traditional political environments, loyalty is often tied to shared policy goals, institutional mission, or party platform. In Trump's orbit, multiple former officials have suggested that loyalty frequently meant allegiance to him individually, publicly, visibly, and without hesitation.

James Comey, former FBI Director, described in congressional testimony and in his memoir that Trump appeared to seek "personal loyalty" rather than professional independence. Comey recounted a private dinner early in the administration during which Trump allegedly said, "I need loyalty, I expect loyalty." Comey later clarified that he offered "honest loyalty," but the episode became emblematic of how Trump framed relationships in personal rather than institutional terms.

John Bolton, who served as National Security Advisor, similarly wrote in his memoir that Trump valued advisers who aligned with him publicly and decisively. Bolton portrayed a decision-making environment in which contradiction was unwelcome, particularly in front of others. While Bolton often framed disagreements in policy terms, his broader account reinforces the pattern: loyalty was not only about executing directives—it was about defending Trump himself.

Michael Cohen has also testified that Trump measured loyalty through willingness to protect him personally, especially during moments of controversy. According to Cohen, public defense during crises was seen as proof of allegiance. Hesitation or nuance could be interpreted as weakness. Cohen's later break with Trump underscored how fragile that loyalty bond could become once personal alignment fractured.

Other former aides, including John Kelly and Anthony Scaramucci, have described an environment where proximity depended heavily on public support. Officials who publicly contradicted or criticized Trump risked rapid marginalization. Praise strengthened position. Silence during controversy could raise suspicion. The metric of loyalty extended beyond policy execution into tone and posture.

Critically, this personalization of loyalty reshaped internal dynamics. When allegiance centers on a leader rather than an institution, disagreement becomes more consequential. Policy debate narrows. Independent judgment can appear threatening. Advisers may self-censor to maintain standing. Over time, this creates a culture where personal allegiance is rewarded more consistently than policy expertise.

The pattern aligns with earlier chapters in Trump's career. In business, former executives described loyalty as survival. In the campaign, aides recounted tests of allegiance. In governance, advisers reported similar expectations. The environment changed from boardroom to White House, but the underlying framework remained stable.

Supporters might argue that strong personal loyalty ensures unity and discipline. Critics contend that equating loyalty with personal allegiance risks undermining institutional norms. Regardless of interpretation, the accounts from former advisers converge on a clear theme: for Trump, loyalty was rarely abstract. It was personal, demonstrable, and central to power.

As the chapter unfolds, this dynamic becomes essential to understanding how Trump maintained control within his party. Leadership, in his model, was not merely about policy direction. It was about allegiance to him.

The Party Recast in His Image

By the close of this chapter, it is evident that Donald Trump did not merely lead the Republican Party—he reshaped it. What began as tension between outsider and establishment evolved into dominance. Skepticism gave way to recalibration. Recalibration hardened into alignment. The party that once questioned him increasingly operated within the framework he defined.

Public shaming replaced quiet persuasion. Endorsements became instruments of enforcement. Dissent narrowed as primary threats grew more credible. Advisors' accounts reveal how loyalty was measured less by policy agreement and more by personal allegiance. The distinction between party loyalty and loyalty to Trump blurred. Institutional authority adjusted to personal authority.

'Trust the person, not the process.'

This transformation altered party norms in profound ways. Leadership became more centralized around personality. Internal disagreement became riskier. Messaging grew more combative. The base, energized and vocal, became both shield and sword—defending

Trump against criticism while disciplining those within the party who deviated.

For Trump, dominating the party was consistent with his broader operating philosophy. Authority must be visible. Loyalty must be public. Opposition must be confronted. The same instincts refined in business, litigation, media, and campaign now operated within party structure. The outsider who once challenged the establishment had become its gravitational center.

Yet dominance within a party is not the same as dominance within a nation. Governing requires navigating institutions that do not bend as easily as campaign structures or partisan ranks. As we move into the next chapter, the focus shifts from party consolidation to governing reality. The question becomes whether a leadership style rooted in confrontation and personal allegiance can function within constitutional boundaries and institutional resistance.

Because once authority is secured, it must be exercised. And exercise, unlike campaign rhetoric, encounters limits.

PART VI – STATEMANSHIP UNDER STRAIN

Chapter 12: Governing as Confrontation

Winning the presidency settled one contest. Governing began another. For Donald Trump, the transition from campaign to office did not signal a change in tone or instinct. The style that had powered his rise—confrontational, personal, and media-driven—did not soften within the constraints of the Oval Office. If anything, the stage grew larger, and the stakes more immediate.

This chapter examines how Trump approached governance not primarily as institutional stewardship, but as continued combat. Political opponents remained adversaries. The press remained hostile. Even elements within the federal bureaucracy were framed as obstacles or part of a "deep state." The campaign's language of grievance and dominance migrated into the mechanics of governing.

Executive orders, public statements, and policy rollouts often unfolded with the urgency and drama of rally speeches. Decisions were announced forcefully. Critics were rebuked publicly. Negotiations with Congress were framed less as collaboration and more as tests of strength. The familiar rhythm persisted: escalation, reaction, amplification.

Governing as confrontation carries consequences. Institutions are built on procedure, continuity, and compromise. Confrontation disrupts those rhythms. It energizes supporters but strains relationships. It simplifies complex policy debates into moral battles. And it transforms oversight into opposition.

In this chapter, we explore how Trump's governing style reflected decades of conditioning—business disputes, litigation strategies, media battles, campaign escalation, party dominance. The same instincts now operated within the constitutional framework of American government.

The question was no longer how to win attention. It was how to wield power.

Because governance tests leadership differently than campaigning does. Campaigns reward energy and intensity. Governing demands durability and negotiation. As we move forward, we will examine how Trump navigated that tension, and whether confrontation, as a governing philosophy, strengthens authority or destabilizes it.

Trump's Transition from Candidate to President

The moment Donald Trump secured the presidency in November 2016, the campaign ended, but the instincts that powered it did not. The transition period offered the first test of whether a confrontational candidate could recalibrate into a governing president. What emerged was less a transformation and more a continuation.

Traditionally, the transition from candidate to president-elect is marked by tone shifts—calls for unity, outreach to former rivals, and careful institutional preparation. Trump did offer gestures of reconciliation, including a White House meeting with President Barack Obama and public statements about serving all Americans. Yet the broader posture remained combative. Claims that the election might be "rigged" gave way to assertions—without evidence—that millions of illegal votes had been cast. Even in victory, grievance language persisted.

The formation of the transition team reflected both disruption and improvisation. Early leadership changes within the transition apparatus signaled volatility. Chris Christie, initially tasked with overseeing transition planning, was replaced by Vice President-elect Mike Pence. Staffing decisions unfolded publicly and sometimes abruptly. The process mirrored campaign dynamics—centralized authority, rapid shifts, and visible internal rivalry.

Cabinet selections combined establishment figures with outsider loyalists. Some appointments reassured Republican leaders; others signaled ideological confrontation. The choices underscored a central tension: Trump was entering the executive branch as both insurgent and incumbent. He would rely on traditional Republican networks while simultaneously challenging Washington norms.

Public communication during this period also retained campaign characteristics. Trump continued using Twitter as a direct channel, commenting on policy, corporations, and media coverage before taking office. Corporate leaders were publicly praised or criticized based on business decisions affecting U.S. jobs. The style was unmistakable—immediate, personalized, and highly visible.

Perhaps most telling was the relationship with the intelligence community and media during the transition. Briefings on foreign interference in the election were met with skepticism and public dispute. Trump's response to press reporting on those assessments reinforced the adversarial dynamic. Instead of defusing tension as president-elect, he escalated it.

Critically, the transition revealed that the campaign mindset had not dissolved. The framing of institutions as hostile persisted. The use of public pressure as leverage continued. The loyalty expectations seen during the campaign followed into the selection of staff and advisers. The presidency was treated not as a reset, but as an expansion of the platform.

Supporters interpreted this continuity as authenticity, proof that Trump would not be absorbed by Washington culture. Critics viewed it as an early warning sign of instability within governance. Both perspectives acknowledged the same reality: the shift from candidate to president did not fundamentally alter Trump's style.

The transition period thus became a preview of governing as confrontation. It demonstrated that the tactics used to win office would not be left behind. Instead, they would be adapted to executive authority. The question now was not whether Trump could command attention—that had been proven. The question was how that command would operate within the structures of power he was about to inherit.

Difficulty Adapting to Institutional Restraint

The presidency differs from campaigning in one critical way: it operates within boundaries. Executive power is significant, but it is constrained by courts, Congress, federal law, bureaucratic process, and constitutional limits. For Donald Trump, whose career had rewarded confrontation and improvisation, these restraints proved persistently frustrating.

Early in his presidency, this tension surfaced in the rollout of major policy initiatives. The first travel ban executive order in January 2017 was signed swiftly and dramatically, fulfilling a campaign promise. Yet its implementation was chaotic, prompting legal challenges and injunctions from federal courts. Instead of treating judicial pushback as routine constitutional review, Trump publicly criticized judges who ruled against the order, labeling one a "so-called judge." The episode revealed a core difficulty: institutional checks were interpreted less as procedural safeguards and more as obstruction.

Relations with Congress displayed similar friction. Trump often expressed impatience with legislative timelines, especially during the effort to repeal and replace the Affordable Care Act. Negotiation within Congress requires coalition-building, compromise, and procedural maneuvering, skills distinct from public pressure. When repeal efforts stalled, Trump frequently criticized members of his own party publicly rather than cultivating quiet consensus. Institutional delay clashed with his preference for rapid, visible victory.

The federal bureaucracy posed another challenge. Presidents rely on agencies staffed by career civil servants who operate within established protocols. Trump repeatedly described segments of this bureaucracy as resistant or disloyal. The term "deep state" entered common usage within his rhetoric and among supporters, reflecting a belief that internal resistance was political rather than structural. Instead of viewing bureaucratic caution as institutional continuity, it was framed as sabotage.

Intelligence agencies and law enforcement institutions became flashpoints as well. Disagreements over assessments of foreign interference, investigations, and oversight processes were frequently aired publicly. Trump's discomfort with independent investigative structures, particularly when they scrutinized his campaign or administration underscored the tension between personal authority and institutional autonomy.

Critically, the constitutional system is designed to slow power. Courts review executive actions. Congress authorizes funding. Agencies implement policy through layered procedures. For a leader accustomed to direct command—whether in business or television—the pace can feel constraining. Trump's public remarks often conveyed impatience with these limits, suggesting that institutional friction was evidence of weakness rather than design.

Supporters argued that his frustration reflected a desire to disrupt inefficiency. Critics contended that it revealed limited appreciation for constitutional balance. Regardless of interpretation, the difficulty adapting to restraint was evident. Governance demanded deference to process. Trump's instincts favored dominance over process.

Over time, this tension became structural. Executive actions were often crafted with an eye toward public messaging as much as legal durability. Judicial setbacks were framed politically. Congressional resistance was personalized. The pattern reinforced confrontation rather than accommodation.

This difficulty adapting to institutional restraint did not arise suddenly in office. It reflected decades of conditioning in environments where escalation often produced results. In the presidency, however, escalation encountered countervailing authority. The collision between personal instinct and constitutional boundary became one of the defining features of Trump's governing style.

Cabinet Turnover and Internal Instability

One of the clearest indicators of governing turbulence during Donald Trump's presidency was the unprecedented level of cabinet and senior staff turnover. While some degree of personnel change is common in any administration, the frequency and visibility of departures during Trump's tenure stood out historically. The pattern reflected not only policy disagreement, but the personalized leadership dynamics described in earlier chapters.

'Next.'

Within the first year alone, several high-profile figures exited or were dismissed. National Security Advisor Michael Flynn resigned weeks into the administration. Press Secretary Sean Spicer departed amid communications turmoil. Chief of Staff Reince Priebus was replaced by John Kelly, who himself later left the role. Secretary of State Rex Tillerson was dismissed via tweet. Defense Secretary Jim Mattis resigned after policy disagreements, particularly over Syria. The list continued across agencies and advisory roles.

The manner of departure often reinforced instability. Some officials learned of their dismissal publicly. Others resigned amid public criticism or escalating tension. Social media announcements sometimes preceded internal briefings. The visibility of these changes signaled that internal conflict was not contained behind closed doors. It played out in real time.

Former officials have described decision-making environments characterized by rapid shifts and competing centers of influence. Steve Bannon, Jared Kushner, and other senior advisers were often reported to hold divergent views on strategy and policy. Rivalries surfaced in media reporting. The atmosphere resembled earlier business accounts— centralized authority with fluctuating proximity to the leader.

Loyalty expectations contributed to the churn. Advisers who publicly contradicted or resisted Trump's direction often found their tenure shortened. Jim Mattis, respected across party lines, resigned after disagreeing with Trump's decision to withdraw troops from Syria, signaling limits to internal dissent. Rex Tillerson reportedly clashed with Trump over diplomatic strategy and was later dismissed. The pattern suggested that alignment with the president's approach was as important as expertise.

High turnover has structural consequences. Policy continuity weakens. Institutional memory fragments. Agency morale declines. Frequent leadership changes complicate coordination across departments. While supporters framed some dismissals as necessary disruption of entrenched bureaucracy, critics argued that instability undermined effective governance.

From a broader perspective, cabinet volatility mirrored campaign and business patterns. Authority remained highly centralized. Decisions could pivot quickly. Loyalty was closely monitored. When friction emerged, resolution often took the form of removal rather than reconciliation.

The cumulative effect was a presidency marked by constant motion. Internal dynamics remained fluid. Public confidence in administrative stability became contested terrain. The executive branch, traditionally a symbol of continuity, appeared reactive and personalized.

Cabinet turnover and internal instability were not isolated management issues. They were reflections of a governing philosophy rooted in confrontation and personal allegiance. The tension between institutional durability and leader-centric authority persisted, and in many ways, defined the operational character of the administration.

Former Officials on Volatility and Impulsiveness

Accounts from former senior officials across multiple departments describe a governing environment shaped by rapid shifts, emotional reaction, and highly personalized decision-making. While supporters often framed this style as flexibility or instinctive leadership, former insiders frequently used different language: volatile, unpredictable, impulsive.

John Kelly, who served as White House Chief of Staff, reportedly told colleagues that managing the flow of information to the president was critical because Trump could react sharply to what he saw on television or read online. According to reporting in outlets such as *The New York Times* and *The Atlantic*, Kelly often attempted to impose structure on decision-making by limiting unscheduled input. The need for such controls, aides suggested, reflected the president's tendency to pivot quickly in response to media narratives.

James Mattis, former Secretary of Defense, described in his resignation letter the importance of alliances and measured strategy—an implicit contrast to what he viewed as abrupt shifts in foreign policy direction. While Mattis maintained a restrained tone publicly, reporting from officials close to the Pentagon indicated that policy announcements, particularly on troop withdrawals, sometimes surprised even senior leadership. The perception that strategic decisions could be declared suddenly without extensive interagency consultation reinforced concerns about impulsiveness.

Rex Tillerson, who served as Secretary of State, was dismissed after months of reported tension. Media accounts described disagreements over diplomatic engagement and North Korea strategy. Tillerson's departure, announced via Twitter before he had been fully briefed, underscored the public and abrupt nature of leadership change. The episode illustrated not only policy divergence but the personalized style of dismissal.

John Bolton, Trump's former National Security Advisor, wrote in his memoir that Trump frequently made decisions based on immediate perception of political advantage rather than structured strategic review. Bolton characterized meetings where foreign policy considerations were discussed through the lens of optics and domestic political reaction. While Bolton's account is critical and contested, it aligns with other officials' descriptions of rapid shifts tied to media cycles.

Anthony Scaramucci, who briefly served as White House Communications Director, described a fast-moving and unpredictable internal culture during his short tenure. Though his time in office was brief, Scaramucci later commented publicly on the speed at which internal dynamics could change and how proximity to the president could evaporate quickly.

Even advisers who remained publicly supportive acknowledged the improvisational character of governance. Decisions were sometimes announced first and refined later. Tweets could reset diplomatic messaging. Policy direction could pivot in response to a cable news segment. The environment demanded constant recalibration from staff.

Critically, volatility does not inherently equate to ineffectiveness. Some leaders embrace rapid decision-making as a form of strength. However, former officials' accounts suggest that the unpredictability within this administration often stemmed less from strategic agility and more from reactive impulse. The centralization of authority around one figure amplified this dynamic. Without strong institutional buffers, mood and media influence carried weight.

These recollections reinforce a through-line from earlier chapters. In business, impulsiveness was described as assertiveness. In campaign, it was framed as authenticity. In governance, it carried broader implications. When decisions affect alliances, markets, and national security, volatility has cascading consequences.

The testimonies of former officials present a portrait consistent with Trump's long-standing style: highly responsive to perceived slights, attentive to media narratives, and inclined toward abrupt shifts when dissatisfied. The presidency did not fundamentally alter that pattern. It magnified it.

Confrontation as a Governing Method

By the end of this chapter, one conclusion becomes unavoidable: Donald Trump did not abandon confrontation when he entered the Oval Office. He institutionalized it. The habits formed in business disputes, sharpened in litigation, amplified through television, and weaponized in campaign rallies followed him into governance. The arena changed. The instinct did not.

The transition from candidate to president revealed continuity rather than recalibration. Institutional restraint—whether from courts, Congress, intelligence agencies, or career officials—was often interpreted not as constitutional design but as resistance. Cabinet turnover reflected an environment where loyalty and alignment outweighed continuity. Former officials' accounts of volatility and impulsiveness reinforced a pattern long visible in earlier chapters.

Governing as confrontation energized supporters who valued disruption over decorum. It signaled strength to those weary of incremental politics. Yet it also strained institutional norms, compressed internal deliberation, and elevated personal allegiance over structural stability. Where campaigns reward escalation, governance tests it. Institutions push back. Courts review. Legislatures stall. Bureaucracies slow.

The presidency became both platform and proving ground. Trump's style did not soften under constraint; it pressed against it. Every legal challenge became a political argument. Every internal disagreement risked public rupture. Every media dispute fed the cycle.

The broader question now emerges: what are the long-term consequences of governing through confrontation? When loyalty is personalized, institutions reframed as adversarial, and dissent narrowed, the immediate objective may be dominance—but the cumulative effect shapes democratic culture itself.

As we move into the next chapter, we examine how this confrontational approach interacted with crisis—moments when unity and institutional coordination are most critical. Because crisis does not reward spectacle in the same way campaigns do. It demands coherence, trust, and sustained governance. And in crisis, leadership style is not performance. It is consequence.

Chapter 13: Eccentricity in Office

Every presidency carries the imprint of personality. But in Donald Trump's case, personality was not a background influence—it was a governing force. Traits that once appeared unconventional in business or entertaining on television took on new weight inside the executive branch. Habits of communication, preference for improvisation, and resistance to traditional restraint shaped not just tone, but outcomes.

This chapter explores the role of eccentricity in Trump's time in office. By eccentricity, we do not mean mere stylistic difference. We refer to patterns that departed from modern presidential norms: spontaneous policy declarations via social media, public disputes with intelligence agencies, abrupt personnel shifts, and a governing rhythm that often prioritized spectacle over process. What once energized rallies now reverberated through institutions.

Presidents have always had distinctive personalities. But Trump's approach blurred the line between public persona and executive function. The improvisational style cultivated in media settings remained visible in diplomatic contexts. The instinct to dominate headlines influenced policy rollout. The preference for loyalty over technocratic expertise shaped staffing decisions.

Supporters viewed this eccentricity as authenticity—proof that he refused to be absorbed by bureaucratic convention. Critics saw instability and erosion of institutional norms. Both perspectives acknowledged the same phenomenon: governance under Trump did not resemble prior administrations in tone or tempo.

In this chapter, we examine how eccentric behavior intersected with executive responsibility. How did unconventional communication affect diplomatic relationships? How did public disputes with officials alter internal morale? How did impulsive messaging interact with global markets and security concerns?

Eccentricity, when attached to private enterprise, carries limited consequence. When attached to the presidency, it carries global implications. As we move forward, we assess not only the visibility of Trump's distinct style, but its structural impact on the office itself. Because personality in power is not ornamental. It is operational.

Erratic Communication Patterns

One of the defining features of Donald Trump's presidency was his communication style—immediate, personal, and often unpredictable. Unlike recent presidents who relied heavily on structured press briefings and carefully vetted statements, Trump frequently communicated directly and spontaneously, particularly through Twitter. The result was a communication pattern that blurred the line between official policy and personal reaction.

Tweets were often issued early in the morning, late at night, or in rapid succession during unfolding events. Some announced policy shifts before agencies had finalized implementation plans. Others criticized allies, foreign leaders, or members of his own administration without prior coordination. Staff frequently learned of major announcements at the same time as the public. This unpredictability created internal strain and required constant recalibration.

For example, sudden declarations regarding troop withdrawals, trade tariffs, or negotiations were sometimes made via social media before formal interagency review had concluded. Markets reacted in real time. Diplomats scrambled to clarify intent. Congressional leaders sought briefings after statements were already public. The pace and tone of communication compressed the space for traditional policy process.

Former officials have described a reactive dynamic. Cable news segments or critical headlines sometimes prompted immediate public response. The cycle became self-perpetuating: media coverage triggered commentary; commentary generated further coverage. The presidency's communication channel operated less as a measured platform and more as a live feed of instinct and counterpunch.

Press briefings also reflected this tension. Contradictions between official statements and presidential tweets occasionally forced aides to reconcile messaging in public. The communications team's role shifted from shaping narrative to managing fallout. Over time, turnover in communications positions reinforced the perception of instability.

Supporters argued that this directness bypassed filtered media interpretation and allowed voters to hear from the president without mediation. They viewed spontaneity as authenticity. Critics countered that erratic messaging undermined diplomatic clarity and weakened institutional credibility. Allies sometimes expressed uncertainty about which statements reflected formal policy and which were rhetorical flourish.

The broader consequence of erratic communication patterns was erosion of predictability. In governance, predictability carries strategic value. Markets respond to signals. Allies rely on consistency. Agencies depend on clear directives. When messaging shifts rapidly or contradicts prior positions, uncertainty spreads.

Trump's communication style did not emerge in office. It was visible in business disputes and campaign rallies. But the scale changed. A tweet from a private citizen carries limited weight. A tweet from a sitting president can move markets, unsettle alliances, or shape national debate within minutes.

Erratic communication became both a tool and a liability. It allowed Trump to dominate headlines and frame narratives instantly. It also amplified volatility and complicated coordination. The presidency, traditionally associated with measured tone and institutional continuity, adopted the rhythm of personal broadcast.

In that shift, communication ceased to be merely descriptive. It became decisive. And when decisiveness operates without filter, governance absorbs the shock.

Public Contradictions and Reversals

Another defining feature of Donald Trump's presidency was the frequency of public contradictions and reversals. Statements made confidently one day were sometimes modified, softened, or directly contradicted the next. In some cases, these reversals followed legal challenges, internal pushback, or international reaction. In others, they appeared to emerge from instinctive recalibration rather than formal review.

'Trust, but... question?'

One prominent example occurred after the 2018 Helsinki summit with Russian President Vladimir Putin. In a joint press conference, Trump appeared to question U.S. intelligence assessments regarding Russian election interference. The remarks generated immediate

143

bipartisan criticism. Within a day, Trump stated that he had misspoken and intended to say he saw no reason Russia "wouldn't" be responsible. The clarification did not erase the initial statement. Instead, it highlighted the speed with which high-stakes comments could be reshaped under pressure.

Trade policy also reflected oscillation. Tariff announcements were sometimes framed as permanent, only to be adjusted after market volatility or negotiation shifts. Deadlines were extended. Rhetoric escalated and softened within short timeframes. Businesses and foreign governments learned to interpret presidential statements cautiously, often waiting for formal documentation before reacting decisively.

On domestic policy, similar patterns appeared. Positions on healthcare repeal strategies shifted during congressional negotiations. Statements regarding the Deferred Action for Childhood Arrivals (DACA) program alternated between hardline enforcement and openness to legislative compromise. Messaging often moved in response to political resistance, judicial rulings, or public reaction.

Former aides have suggested that Trump viewed reversals not as inconsistencies but as tactical flexibility. In business negotiation, shifting position can be leverage. In governance, however, public contradiction carries different consequences. When policy signals change rapidly, credibility becomes fragile. Allies question durability. Opponents test boundaries. Agencies struggle to implement direction that may pivot unexpectedly.

Press briefings frequently became exercises in interpretation. Spokespersons clarified, reframed, or contextualized earlier statements. At times, official documents did not fully align with prior remarks. The gap between rhetoric and policy widened, forcing observers to distinguish between symbolic language and actionable directive.

Supporters often framed reversals as evidence that Trump was responsive rather than rigid. They argued that adaptation demonstrated pragmatism. Critics saw inconsistency and lack of preparation. The debate itself became part of the political spectacle.

What is clear is that public contradiction altered the rhythm of governance. Predictability, traditionally valued in diplomacy and economic planning, became less reliable. Markets responded not only to policy decisions but to tone. Foreign leaders weighed whether statements represented final position or opening gambit.

Over time, this pattern reshaped expectations. Analysts began parsing tweets and rally remarks with caution, looking for confirmation before assuming policy shift. The presidency adopted a fluid narrative style, one in which statements could be emphatic without being enduring.

Public contradictions and reversals did not exist in isolation. They were part of a broader governing style rooted in immediacy and dominance of the news cycle. Yet when the presidency speaks, the world listens. And when that speech shifts quickly, uncertainty travels just as fast.

Erratic Private Meetings

While public communication often drew the most attention, former officials have suggested that volatility was not confined to tweets or rallies. Several aides have described private meetings in which discussions could become erratic, circular, or narrowly fixated on specific grievances. These accounts, drawn from memoirs, congressional testimony, and investigative reporting, paint a picture of a decision-making environment shaped heavily by mood, media narratives, and personal preoccupation.

John Bolton, who served as National Security Advisor, wrote in *The Room Where It Happened* that policy meetings sometimes veered unexpectedly from structured agenda to tangential concerns. Bolton described instances in which strategic discussions returned repeatedly to perceived slights, media narratives, or personal rivalries. While Bolton's account reflects his own perspective and has been contested by Trump, it aligns with other officials' descriptions of meetings that could drift away from policy architecture and toward political optics.

Fiona Hill, a senior National Security Council official, testified before Congress that certain conversations with the president reflected an intense focus on specific political narratives. During impeachment hearings, Hill described how policy deliberations concerning Ukraine became intertwined with domestic political concerns. Her testimony suggested that the boundaries between governance and personal political interest were sometimes blurred in closed-door discussions.

Former Chief of Staff John Kelly reportedly told associates that meetings required careful management because topics could escalate quickly. According to reporting in *The New York Times*, Kelly sought to impose structured briefing documents and limit extraneous input, believing that unmanaged conversation risked digression or impulsive reaction. The need for such controls indicated awareness among senior staff of how meetings could shift direction abruptly.

Several aides have also described fixation on individual media stories or personal criticisms. According to Michael Cohen's testimony and later interviews, Trump often entered discussions focused on negative press coverage and sought identification of the source. Conversations that began with policy matters could pivot toward grievances about journalists or political opponents. While such focus may reflect the pressures of public office, aides suggested that the intensity of these reactions shaped the tone of broader deliberations.

National security discussions, according to some accounts, were not immune to this pattern. Jim Mattis and other defense officials reportedly emphasized strategic continuity and alliance stability, while Trump frequently returned to cost-sharing concerns and transactional framing.

Meetings sometimes revolved around financial contribution metrics rather than long-term geopolitical alignment. Supporters viewed this as pragmatic negotiation; critics viewed it as narrow framing.

Another recurring description from former staff concerned repetition. Some aides reported that certain themes—crowd sizes, perceived electoral legitimacy, loyalty of subordinates—surfaced repeatedly in private meetings. This repetition could crowd out time allocated for detailed policy briefings. In high-pressure environments where decision-making windows are limited, fixation on symbolic issues may redirect institutional focus.

It is important to note that accounts vary. Supporters within the administration have argued that Trump's meeting style was conversational and flexible rather than chaotic. They describe an environment in which open discussion allowed candid input. However, even sympathetic voices acknowledge that conversations could pivot rapidly, requiring advisers to adapt in real time.

The broader implication of these accounts lies in how decision-making culture shapes governance. In structured administrations, meetings often follow agenda, briefing materials, and defined objectives. When discussions become erratic or fixation-driven, policy development may become reactive rather than strategic. Staff energy shifts toward managing volatility rather than refining implementation.

These descriptions echo patterns visible throughout Trump's career. In business settings, former executives described rapid mood shifts. In campaign environments, aides recounted reactive messaging. In office, those same tendencies operated within institutions responsible for national security, economic stability, and diplomatic continuity.

Private meetings are rarely fully visible to the public. Yet they form the core of executive governance. When aides describe those meetings as erratic or dominated by recurring grievances, they raise questions about how priorities are set and sustained. In a presidency where personality already played a central role, the tone of private deliberation mattered deeply.

Ultimately, these accounts suggest that eccentricity in office was not limited to public spectacle. It extended into internal process. And when internal process reflects unpredictability or fixation, the ripple effects move outward, into policy clarity, institutional morale, and national direction.

Eccentric Traits Hardened under the Pressures of Office

Personality traits that appear manageable in private enterprise can intensify when exposed to the relentless pressure of the presidency. For Donald Trump, tendencies toward confrontation, sensitivity to criticism, improvisational communication, and fixation on loyalty did not soften once in office. Under scrutiny, they often became more pronounced.

The presidency amplifies every stimulus. Media coverage is constant. Opposition is organized. Legal oversight is formalized. In such an environment, leaders either absorb institutional rhythm or push back against it. In Trump's case, former aides and observers have suggested that pressure reinforced his existing instincts rather than moderating them.

Criticism, for example, did not gradually fade into background noise. It became central to daily engagement. Impeachment inquiries, special counsel investigations, and relentless media scrutiny intensified the perception of being under siege. Trump's response was not withdrawal but escalation. Public rhetoric sharpened. Language toward opponents grew more absolute. The sense of personal grievance expanded into governing narrative.

Communication patterns also hardened. Rather than adopting a more restrained tone as global stakes increased, Trump continued to rely on immediate, personal messaging. Social media remained a primary outlet. Where prior presidents often narrowed public communication during crises to project stability, Trump frequently amplified commentary. The platform that once built political momentum became a tool for counterattack in office.

Internal loyalty expectations intensified under pressure. As controversies mounted, visible allegiance from advisers became more important. Officials who contradicted or distanced themselves publicly often exited. The circle tightened. In high-pressure environments, leaders often seek trusted confidants. In Trump's case, that search for trust sometimes narrowed the diversity of internal perspective.

Eccentric traits also intersected with crisis management. During moments of national tension, whether diplomatic confrontation or domestic unrest, the preference for dominance over deliberation remained evident. Briefings sometimes became public debates. Press conferences evolved into combative exchanges. The boundary between crisis communication and campaign rhetoric thinned.

Supporters argued that this hardening reflected resilience. They saw a president unwilling to bend under institutional hostility. Critics interpreted it as entrenchment – evidence that exposure to constraint deepened resistance to it. Both interpretations acknowledge that pressure did not produce moderation. It produced consolidation of style.

There is a psychological dimension to this process. Under sustained challenge, individuals often revert to core habits. The presidency did not create Trump's eccentric traits. It tested them. And in that test, traits such as impulsiveness, defensiveness, and media fixation did not dissipate. They crystallized.

The result was a governing style increasingly defined by continuity with earlier chapters of his life. The businessman who counterpunched critics, the candidate who escalated under attack, the party leader who demanded visible loyalty—all were present in the presidency. Institutional pressure did not smooth the edges. It sharpened them.

As the chapter unfolds, this hardening becomes central to understanding later developments. Because once eccentricity solidifies under pressure, adaptation becomes less likely. And in the executive branch, hardened traits shape not only rhetoric but consequence.

Personality as Policy Force

By the end of this chapter, we see clearly that eccentricity in Donald Trump's presidency was not cosmetic. It was structural. Communication patterns, public contradictions, fixation in private meetings, and hardened instincts under pressure all point to the same reality: personality did not orbit power, it directed it.

Erratic messaging blurred the line between reaction and policy. Public reversals created uncertainty in diplomatic and economic arenas. Private meetings described as fixation-driven revealed how personal grievance and media narratives could shape institutional deliberation. Under sustained scrutiny, traits that once appeared unconventional hardened into governing reflex.

"Double down."

Supporters viewed this as authenticity under siege. Critics saw destabilization of norms. But regardless of interpretation, the effect was undeniable. The presidency adopted the cadence of immediacy. Predictability weakened. Institutional restraint was met with confrontation rather than adaptation.

What distinguishes this phase from earlier chapters is scale. In business, eccentricity could disrupt a project. In campaign, it could energize a crowd. In office, it affected global markets, alliances, and public trust. Personality became policy force. Tone influenced treaty negotiations. Tweets moved financial indices. Press conferences altered diplomatic posture.

The cumulative impact reshaped expectations of executive conduct. What once might have been considered deviation became routine. Norms adjusted. Boundaries shifted. The presidency became a live broadcast of temperament as much as administration.

As we move forward, the focus widens beyond style to consequence. Because governing is measured not only by tone, but by legacy. Institutions absorb shock. Allies recalibrate. Voters reassess. The next chapter examines how these patterns intersected with moments of national and global crisis, when leadership style is tested not by opposition alone, but by events beyond control.

Chapter 14: The Press, the Courts, and the Perpetual Enemy

From the earliest days of his presidency, Donald Trump did not merely clash with institutions—he cast them as adversaries. The press was not just critical; it was "fake." Courts were not simply exercising review; they were obstructing the will of the people. Investigations were not oversight; they were witch hunts. The language of conflict became constant, and over time, institutional friction evolved into a permanent battlefield.

This chapter examines how Trump framed the press, the judiciary, and other oversight mechanisms as perpetual enemies rather than coequal components of democratic governance. While tension between presidents and institutions is not new, the intensity and personalization of this confrontation marked a departure from recent norms. Disagreement was reframed as hostility. Accountability was reframed as sabotage.

We explore how media criticism became proof of bias, how judicial rulings became political affronts, and how investigative bodies were portrayed as extensions of partisan opposition. In this framework, institutions were not independent checks; they were actors within an adversarial narrative. Conflict was not episodic. It was ongoing.

The strategic dimension is clear. Casting institutions as adversaries mobilizes supporters and consolidates loyalty. It simplifies complex constitutional dynamics into moral struggle. But the structural implications are equally significant. Democratic systems rely on tension balanced by mutual legitimacy. When legitimacy erodes, tension escalates.

As we move through this chapter, we assess not only Trump's rhetoric, but its cumulative impact. How does repeated institutional confrontation shape public trust? What happens when courts and press are framed as political enemies rather than constitutional partners? And how does perpetual conflict alter the boundaries between executive authority and democratic accountability?

The presidency has always required negotiation with independent institutions. Under Trump, negotiation often gave way to narrative warfare. The question now is not whether conflict existed—but how constant confrontation reshaped the relationship between power and restraint.

Trump's Adversarial Stance toward Oversight

Oversight is built into the architecture of American democracy. Congress investigates. Inspectors general audit. Courts review executive action. The press scrutinizes decisions and exposes misconduct. These mechanisms are designed not to weaken the presidency, but to restrain and legitimize it. Under Donald Trump, however, oversight was frequently framed not as constitutional function but as political aggression.

From early in his presidency, Trump described investigations into his campaign and administration as partisan attacks. The special counsel inquiry led by Robert Mueller was repeatedly labeled a "witch hunt." Rather than acknowledge oversight as routine in matters involving national security and election interference, Trump cast the investigation as an attempt to delegitimize his victory. The language escalated tension and personalized what had historically been institutional process.

Congressional oversight followed a similar trajectory. When the House of Representatives initiated impeachment proceedings, Trump framed the effort not as constitutional review but as a coup attempt. The rhetoric intensified divisions, positioning oversight as existential threat rather than procedural mechanism. Supporters were mobilized around the idea that investigation itself was evidence of corruption within the opposition.

Inspectors general, whose mandate is to ensure accountability within executive agencies, also faced resistance. Several were removed or criticized publicly after overseeing inquiries into administration conduct. While presidents have authority over such appointments, the pattern of public rebuke reinforced the perception that scrutiny was unwelcome.

Judicial review—another cornerstone of oversight—triggered sharp response when rulings delayed or blocked executive actions. Instead of accepting adverse decisions as part of legal process, Trump frequently criticized individual judges. Public statements questioned their legitimacy or political motives. The tension between executive authority and judicial independence became a recurring public spectacle.

The press, functioning as informal oversight through investigation and reporting, was treated as a primary antagonist. Negative coverage was framed as deliberate misinformation. The term "enemy of the people" was used to describe segments of the media. This phrasing, historically charged, intensified the adversarial framing of oversight bodies.

Supporters argued that Trump was confronting what they viewed as entrenched institutional bias. They saw oversight bodies and media organizations as aligned against him. Critics argued that delegitimizing oversight mechanisms weakened democratic guardrails and eroded public trust in independent institutions.

What distinguishes Trump's stance is not that he resisted oversight— many presidents have done so—but the consistency and intensity with which it was framed as hostile. Oversight was rarely acknowledged as structural necessity. It was depicted as partisan conspiracy or bureaucratic sabotage.

This adversarial posture reshaped the public narrative around accountability. When investigations are cast as attacks, their findings become easier to dismiss. When courts are framed as political actors, their rulings lose perceived neutrality. When the press is labeled dishonest, its reporting loses credibility among segments of the population.

Oversight and executive authority exist in deliberate tension. That tension is a stabilizing feature of democratic governance. Under Trump, the tension did not dissipate—it escalated. And as escalation became routine, the relationship between power and restraint grew more combative, setting the stage for even sharper institutional confrontations in the chapters ahead.

Legal Aides' Perspectives on Resistance to Constraints

Among the most revealing accounts of Donald Trump's governing style come from former legal advisers who worked at the intersection of executive power and constitutional restraint. Lawyers within the White House and the Department of Justice are tasked not only with defending presidential authority, but with delineating its limits. Several of those who served during Trump's presidency later described persistent tension between legal constraint and presidential impulse.

Donald McGahn, who served as White House Counsel, reportedly viewed his role as protecting the presidency from legal overreach, including overreach by the president himself. According to testimony and reporting during the special counsel investigation, McGahn resisted certain directives that he believed could create legal jeopardy, including efforts related to the dismissal of Special Counsel Robert Mueller. McGahn later cooperated with investigators, describing instances in which he perceived pressure to act in ways that might obstruct inquiry. His stance reflected a traditional view of the counsel's office: to serve the institution, not merely the individual.

Attorney General William Barr offered a more complex example. While often publicly supportive of executive authority, Barr's memoir and interviews suggest moments of friction. He defended broad presidential powers but expressed concern when public statements undermined Department of Justice credibility. Barr reportedly resisted suggestions that the Department pursue investigations perceived as politically motivated. His eventual resignation followed growing tension, particularly after he stated publicly that the Department had found no evidence of widespread election fraud sufficient to change the 2020 outcome.

Pat Cipollone, who succeeded McGahn as White House Counsel, also navigated moments of acute institutional tension. During impeachment proceedings, Cipollone defended the president vigorously. Yet reporting later indicated that in the final weeks of the administration, he cautioned against certain proposals to challenge electoral certification in ways that might violate constitutional boundaries. His position reflected the recurring dilemma faced by legal aides: balancing loyalty to the president with duty to legal framework.

Former Acting Attorney General Jeffrey Rosen and senior Justice Department officials likewise described resisting pressure to endorse claims of election fraud unsupported by evidence. Public testimony before Congress revealed that internal legal leadership pushed back against attempts to use the Department to validate political narratives. These accounts underscored that within the executive branch, not all resistance originated externally; it sometimes emerged from within.

Across these perspectives, a consistent theme appears: Trump often viewed legal limitations as obstacles rather than guardrails. Advisers who urged caution sometimes framed their counsel as protection against long-term institutional damage. In several reported instances, lawyers documented conversations or insisted on procedural formality, aware of potential legal exposure.

Supporters of Trump have argued that robust executive authority requires aggressive assertion, especially in the face of political opposition. Critics contend that the presidency's strength lies precisely in adherence to constitutional limits. Legal aides found themselves mediating between those philosophies.

The friction between impulse and restraint did not always produce rupture. In many cases, legal structures ultimately held. Executive actions were revised. Directives were not issued. Yet the frequency of such moments suggests that resistance to constraints was not incidental—it was structural.

Legal advisers occupy a unique vantage point. They witness both the ambition of executive authority and the boundaries imposed by law. Their accounts reveal a presidency often pressing against those boundaries, testing their elasticity. In doing so, Trump's administration highlighted a fundamental tension at the heart of executive power: how far it can stretch before it strains the constitutional fabric designed to contain it.

Framing Accountability as Persecution

Throughout Donald Trump's presidency, one of the most consistent rhetorical strategies was reframing accountability mechanisms as acts of persecution. Investigations, legal challenges, impeachment proceedings, and media scrutiny were not acknowledged as routine components of democratic oversight. Instead, they were portrayed as coordinated attempts to undermine, delegitimize, or destroy his presidency.

The special counsel investigation into Russian election interference became the earliest and most sustained example. Trump repeatedly labeled it a "witch hunt," a phrase loaded with historical imagery of unjust accusation and moral panic. By casting the inquiry in these terms, he shifted the narrative from legal examination to political victimhood. The language suggested not merely disagreement, but targeted injustice.

This framing intensified during impeachment proceedings. Rather than engage primarily on the substance of allegations, Trump described the process as a "coup" or partisan assault. Public statements emphasized betrayal and sabotage rather than constitutional review. The message to supporters was clear: accountability was not oversight; it was persecution by entrenched enemies unwilling to accept his legitimacy.

Legal actions against associates were similarly absorbed into this narrative. Indictments or convictions of close aides were described as collateral damage in a broader campaign against him. The implication was that proximity to Trump invited unjust targeting. In this framing, law enforcement institutions became political actors rather than neutral enforcers.

The rhetorical shift carried strategic advantage. When accountability is cast as persecution, evidence becomes secondary to motive. Critics are not simply mistaken; they are malicious. Supporters are mobilized not around policy debate, but around defense. The leader's personal jeopardy becomes collective cause.

Framing oversight as persecution also creates insulation. If every investigation is politically motivated, then unfavorable findings can be dismissed without substantive rebuttal. The logic becomes self-reinforcing: investigation proves hostility; hostility proves bias; bias invalidates investigation. Institutional legitimacy erodes within that loop.

This approach was not entirely new in Trump's career. In business disputes and media conflicts, he often portrayed legal challenges as unfair targeting. In office, however, the scale changed dramatically. The presidency occupies a constitutional role subject to formal review. When that review is reframed as attack, public trust in institutional balance can weaken.

Supporters argued that Trump was confronting what they viewed as politically weaponized institutions. Critics contended that casting accountability as persecution undermined democratic norms and encouraged institutional mistrust. The divide reflected broader polarization, but the rhetorical pattern remained constant.

The significance of this framing lies in its durability. Even after formal processes concluded, whether investigations ended or impeachments resolved, the narrative of persecution persisted. It became part of political identity, reinforcing the idea that resistance to Trump was not principled disagreement but existential opposition.

In a democracy, accountability mechanisms are designed to preserve legitimacy through scrutiny. When scrutiny is recast as persecution, legitimacy itself becomes contested. Under Trump, this reframing became a central tool, not only for defense, but for mobilization. And once accountability is interpreted as attack, the boundaries between governance and grievance grow increasingly thin.

Reinforcement of Siege Mentality

Over time, the repeated framing of oversight as persecution and institutions as hostile forces contributed to what can best be described as a siege mentality. A siege mentality does not simply involve facing opposition. It involves interpreting opposition as coordinated, existential, and relentless. Under Donald Trump's presidency, this outlook became both rhetorical posture and governing lens.

The language was consistent. The media was "out to get" him. The courts were obstructing him. Intelligence agencies were aligned against him. Political opponents were not merely competing; they were conspiring. The accumulation of investigations, leaks, and impeachment proceedings reinforced the narrative that he, and by extension his supporters, were under constant attack.

This framing did more than mobilize a base. It reshaped internal decision-making. When leaders believe they are under siege, they prioritize loyalty and rapid defense. Trust narrows. Dissent becomes suspect. Outside information is filtered through suspicion. Former aides have suggested that criticism was often interpreted not as constructive challenge but as confirmation of hostility.

'UNDER ATTACK.'

The siege mentality also blurred lines between governance and campaign. Rally-style rhetoric continued well into the presidency, reinforcing the sense of ongoing struggle. Political opponents were framed less as alternative policymakers and more as threats to national survival. The country was depicted as being taken from its rightful direction by corrupt elites and shadowy forces.

Public disputes with institutions intensified the perception. Judicial rulings were described as political. Media investigations were dismissed as fabrications. Congressional oversight was cast as sabotage. Each new development was integrated into a broader narrative of encirclement. The presidency became less about administration and more about resistance.

Critically, siege mentality strengthens cohesion among loyalists. Shared perception of threat builds solidarity. Supporters rally more fiercely when they believe their leader is targeted unfairly. The narrative of "us against them" simplifies complex political dynamics into moral clarity. Loyalty deepens under pressure.

However, siege mentality also narrows strategic flexibility. When criticism is interpreted as attack, compromise appears dangerous. Institutions are viewed as adversarial rather than coequal. The capacity for bipartisan negotiation diminishes. Governance becomes defensive rather than collaborative.

This mindset did not arise in isolation. It reflected long-standing patterns in Trump's personal and professional history—turning disputes into existential conflicts, elevating criticism into betrayal, and using confrontation as proof of authenticity. In office, however, the consequences were amplified. The presidency is designed to operate within a web of independent institutions. When those institutions are treated as enemy encampments, tension becomes structural.

The reinforcement of siege mentality thus marked a pivotal shift. It transformed episodic conflicts into continuous narrative. It bound supporters more tightly to the leader. And it deepened polarization between branches of government and segments of the public.

In a constitutional system, friction between power and oversight is inevitable. But when friction is interpreted as siege, governance evolves into perpetual defense. And in perpetual defense, trust once eroded is difficult to restore.

The Architecture of Permanent Conflict

By the end of this chapter, a pattern stands unmistakably clear. Donald Trump did not treat oversight as a structural feature of democracy. He treated it as opposition. The press was not an independent check but an adversary. The courts were not constitutional arbiters but obstacles. Investigations were not review but persecution. In this reframing, accountability became attack.

Legal aides described efforts to impose restraint as protective necessity. Judicial rulings triggered public rebuke. Congressional oversight was absorbed into a narrative of sabotage. Each instance of scrutiny reinforced a broader storyline of encirclement. Over time, the presidency operated within a state of permanent conflict—not episodic disagreement, but sustained confrontation.

Framing accountability as persecution strengthened political loyalty but weakened institutional trust. Reinforcing a siege mentality mobilized supporters but narrowed space for compromise. The language of hostility transformed constitutional friction into moral warfare. Institutions designed to balance power became characters in an adversarial narrative.

This shift did not occur in isolation. It was consistent with patterns visible across Trump's life—business disputes framed as betrayal, media criticism framed as injustice, party dissent framed as disloyalty. The presidency did not create the instinct. It magnified it.

The deeper consequence lies not only in specific conflicts, but in normalization. When press scrutiny is routinely labeled corrupt, public confidence fractures. When judicial review is portrayed as partisan, neutrality erodes. When oversight is equated with persecution, constitutional design is recast as conspiracy.

Yet conflict alone does not define governance. It shapes response. It shapes memory. It shapes political culture. As we move into the next chapter, we turn to the ultimate test of leadership under strain: national crisis. Because crisis compresses time and demands trust. And in crisis, institutions must function not as enemies, but as instruments of coordination.

The question that follows is not whether conflict persists. It is whether a presidency built on perpetual confrontation can pivot when unity becomes indispensable.

PART VII – CHARACTER AS CONSEQUENCE

Chapter 15: The Psychology of Power

Power does not merely reveal character. It intensifies it. By the time Donald Trump entered the presidency, the traits that defined his business career, media presence, and political ascent had already hardened under scrutiny and success. But executive authority introduced something new: permanence of influence. Decisions were no longer confined to deals or campaigns. They carried national and global consequence.

This chapter moves beyond chronology and into psychology. It asks not only what Trump did in power, but how power interacted with his personality. How did decades of confrontation, affirmation, grievance, and dominance shape his self-perception once he occupied the highest office? How did public validation—or public resistance—alter the way he interpreted challenge? And how did the psychological rewards of visibility influence governing behavior?

Throughout earlier chapters, we have traced consistent patterns: sensitivity to criticism, preference for loyalty, instinctive escalation, reliance on spectacle, and framing of conflict as existential. In the presidency, these tendencies operated at maximum scale. Applause was louder. Opposition was sharper. Stakes were higher. The psychological environment was amplified.

Power can stabilize leaders by forcing discipline. It can also reinforce instincts by removing constraint. For Trump, the presidency became both validation and battleground. Each victory confirmed narrative. Each challenge intensified defense. The interplay between external pressure and internal response shaped not just policy decisions, but tone and posture.

In this chapter, we explore the feedback loop between authority and identity. How did affirmation from supporters reinforce confidence?

How did resistance from institutions deepen grievance? How did the constant spotlight affect impulse control and decision-making rhythm?

Understanding the psychology of power does not excuse action. It explains pattern. Leadership at this level is not only strategic. It is deeply personal. And when personality and power converge, the result defines legacy.

As we proceed, we examine whether the presidency tempered instinct or magnified it. Because in the final measure, power does not transform personality in isolation. It interacts with it. And that interaction determines how history remembers both.

Patterns of Narcissism, Insecurity, and Retribution

Across memoirs, interviews, and congressional testimony, several of Donald Trump's former associates have described recurring psychological patterns they observed at close range—intense need for affirmation, sensitivity to criticism, and a strong impulse toward retaliation. These descriptions vary in tone and motive, and many come from individuals who later broke with Trump. Still, certain themes appear consistently across accounts.

Michael Cohen, Trump's longtime personal attorney, testified before Congress that Trump was "a man who would not hesitate to lie to protect himself" and described a leader highly focused on image and loyalty. Cohen portrayed Trump as deeply attentive to how he was perceived publicly, particularly in media coverage. According to Cohen, negative headlines could dominate internal discussion, sometimes overshadowing substantive policy matters. While Cohen's relationship with Trump deteriorated significantly, his description of image preoccupation echoes other accounts.

Omarosa Manigault Newman, who worked in both the campaign and the White House, described in her memoir an environment where praise was welcomed and criticism was met with hostility. She wrote that Trump required consistent affirmation and reacted sharply when he felt slighted. Though her account is controversial and contested by Trump, it aligns with earlier business-era descriptions of demand for visible loyalty.

John Bolton and other senior officials suggested in their writings that Trump's self-conception as uniquely capable shaped his approach to disagreement. Bolton described meetings where Trump emphasized personal instinct over expert consensus, particularly in foreign policy contexts. Critics interpret this as narcissistic confidence; supporters see it as decisive leadership. The distinction often rests on interpretation of motive rather than observation of behavior.

James Comey, in his memoir and testimony, described interactions that he interpreted as requests for personal loyalty rather than institutional integrity. Comey characterized Trump as seeking affirmation and allegiance from law enforcement leadership. Whether one accepts Comey's interpretation or not, the episode contributed to broader discussion about personalization of authority.

Another recurring theme in associates' accounts is retribution. Former aides have described a pattern in which critics, whether media figures, former staff, or political opponents, were targeted publicly after voicing dissent. Nicknames, social media criticism, and rally remarks often followed high-profile disagreements. This retaliatory style was not confined to politics; it had been visible in Trump's business disputes decades earlier.

Insecurity is more difficult to measure directly, but several former officials have suggested that sensitivity to status markers—crowd sizes, television ratings, poll numbers—indicated strong investment in public validation. Reports of intense reaction to perceived diminishment, such as comparisons to predecessors or unfavorable coverage, reinforce this impression. The attention to optics often appeared deeply personal rather than merely strategic.

It is important to note that psychological labeling carries risk of oversimplification. Diagnoses require clinical evaluation, not political commentary. However, when close associates independently describe patterns—intense need for admiration, hypersensitivity to criticism, and retaliatory response to dissent—those patterns become analytically relevant.

Supporters frequently interpret these traits differently. They argue that confidence mistaken for narcissism is necessary for leadership. They view counterattack as strength rather than insecurity. They frame retaliation as refusal to be bullied by entrenched interests. The divergence in interpretation reflects broader polarization.

Yet regardless of viewpoint, the cumulative testimony suggests that personal psychology played a central role in Trump's governing style. Praise energized. Criticism provoked. Loyalty was prized. Dissent triggered response. These dynamics shaped relationships within the administration, interactions with Congress, and engagement with the media.

In high office, personality is not abstract. It influences staffing, negotiation, and crisis response. When associates describe patterns of narcissism, insecurity, and retribution, they are describing not just temperament but operational consequence. And in the presidency, operational consequence defines impact.

How Success and Survival Reinforced Maladaptive Traits

One of the most consequential dynamics in Donald Trump's career is that behaviors widely criticized as impulsive, confrontational, or excessive were often followed by survival or even victory. In psychological terms, reinforcement matters. When a pattern produces reward, it tends to harden rather than soften. Across business, media, campaign, and presidency, Trump experienced repeated cycles in which escalation led not to collapse, but to endurance.

In the 1990s, after near insolvency and corporate bankruptcies tied to casinos and leveraged projects, Trump did not disappear from public life. He renegotiated debt, retained brand visibility, and eventually reemerged through licensing and television. The lesson was clear: aggressive negotiation and public confidence could outlast structural crisis. Survival validated instinct.

In media conflicts, counterattack often shifted narrative momentum. Rather than retreat under criticism, Trump doubled down. Lawsuits, public denunciations, and combative interviews kept him central to the story. Attention—even negative attention—maintained relevance. Over time, that relevance became asset.

The 2016 campaign reinforced the pattern at historic scale. Statements that critics predicted would end his candidacy instead amplified his support among key voter blocs. Controversies generated coverage. Coverage solidified base loyalty. Electoral victory validated the approach. If escalation had been risky, it was now rewarded with the presidency.

Once in office, impeachment proceedings and investigations followed. Yet Trump survived those as well. The Senate did not remove him from office. Support within his party largely held. From a behavioral standpoint, the message was consistent: confrontation did not produce disqualification. It produced consolidation.

Psychologists often describe maladaptive traits as patterns that create short-term advantage but long-term cost. Traits such as hypersensitivity to criticism, retaliatory impulse, and need for dominance may destabilize relationships, yet they can also generate short-term leverage in competitive environments. In Trump's case, environments repeatedly rewarded forceful assertion over restraint.

Success under pressure can entrench belief in personal infallibility. If critics are overcome and institutions withstand challenge without removing authority, the internal narrative strengthens: instinct works. Escalation works. Loyalty enforcement works. Survival becomes proof of correctness.

Close associates have suggested that each victory reinforced confidence in confrontation as default strategy. When challenges were reframed as persecution and endured, grievance deepened rather than diminished. When electoral outcomes defied polling predictions, skepticism toward expert consensus intensified.

It is important to distinguish between resilience and reinforcement. Resilience allows adaptation. Reinforcement can discourage it. In Trump's trajectory, repeated survival reduced incentive to recalibrate. Institutional pushback did not produce moderation; it often produced counter-escalation.

Supporters interpret this pattern as strength—evidence of a leader who withstands relentless opposition. Critics see entrenchment— confirmation that feedback loops failed to correct excess. Both perspectives acknowledge that outcomes matter. In politics especially, survival reshapes psychology.

By the later stages of his presidency, the cumulative effect was visible. Traits once tactical became structural. Confidence hardened into certainty. Retaliation became routine. The belief that challenge equals hostility solidified. Success and survival had not tempered instinct. They had affirmed it.

In power, reinforcement shapes legacy. When behavior produces victory, the lesson endures long after the moment passes. And in Trump's case, the arc of success and survival repeatedly signaled that confrontation was not liability; it was method.

Lack of Course Correction Over Decades

When examining Donald Trump's trajectory from young developer to president, one striking pattern emerges: the remarkable consistency of his behavioral approach across decades. While most public figures evolve—tempering tone, adjusting strategy, absorbing institutional norms—Trump's core instincts remained largely unchanged. Confrontation, personal loyalty, media fixation, retaliatory impulse, and preference for dominance over collaboration appear in the 1980s as clearly as they do in the 2010s.

In the early business years, former contractors and executives described a management style centered on control and public positioning. Legal conflict was common. Disputes were escalated rather than quietly resolved. Public image was carefully cultivated, and criticism was aggressively countered. Financial setbacks did not prompt visible philosophical reassessment. Instead, they produced rebranding and renewed assertion.

The transition into licensing and television did not significantly alter that posture. If anything, it amplified it. *The Apprentice* rewarded decisive rhetoric and public elimination. The show reinforced a leadership model rooted in personal authority rather than collaborative governance. There is little evidence from that period of ideological moderation or structural recalibration. Success validated the model.

During the 2016 campaign, patterns visible in business—escalation under criticism, branding over policy depth, public shaming of opponents—reappeared almost unchanged. Political resistance did not soften tone. It intensified it. The campaign environment rewarded forcefulness, further reducing incentive for introspection or strategic restraint.

Even in the presidency, where institutional constraint and global responsibility traditionally moderate executive behavior, Trump's foundational traits remained intact. Judicial setbacks prompted criticism of judges rather than adaptation of rhetoric. Congressional resistance elicited public rebuke rather than sustained coalition-building. Cabinet turnover reflected continuity with earlier loyalty-based management.

Course correction typically follows failure or sustained negative consequence. In Trump's case, setbacks were often reframed as unfair treatment. Investigations were persecution. Media criticism was bias. Electoral victories were validation. Survival after impeachment reinforced resilience rather than reconsideration. The psychological incentive to adjust diminished when confrontation repeatedly yielded endurance.

Former aides have suggested that self-reflection was limited. Critics were dismissed as enemies. Departing officials were labeled disloyal. Dissenting perspectives rarely translated into visible recalibration. Instead, the pattern was continuity—assert, counterattack, consolidate support.

Supporters interpret this consistency as authenticity. They argue that Trump's refusal to bend demonstrates principle and resolve. Critics view the same pattern as rigidity – an inability or unwillingness to adapt to changing institutional realities. Regardless of interpretation, the historical through-line is evident.

Over decades, environments shifted dramatically, from private real estate markets to global diplomacy. Yet the operating style remained recognizably similar. This lack of course correction suggests a deeply entrenched leadership identity. Adaptation, when it occurred, was tactical rather than psychological. Messaging adjusted; instinct did not.

The long arc of Trump's career reveals not a leader shaped by institutions, but one who sought to shape institutions to fit preexisting instincts. That consistency is central to understanding his impact. In political life, evolution often signals maturation. In Trump's case, repetition signals conviction.

Whether that conviction represents steadfastness or inflexibility is a matter of perspective. What is clear is that across business, media, campaign, and presidency, course correction was minimal. The same traits that defined his ascent defined his governance. And when leadership patterns remain unchanged across decades, their consequences compound.

Power Did Not Transform, It Confirmed

By the close of this chapter, a central insight emerges: power did not fundamentally change Donald Trump. It confirmed him. The patterns described by close associates—need for affirmation, sensitivity to criticism, retaliatory impulse—were not fleeting traits of campaign intensity. They were durable characteristics reinforced across decades.

'I was right.'

Success did not moderate instinct. It validated it. Financial survival after near collapse reinforced confrontation as strategy. Media prominence reinforced spectacle as leverage. Electoral victory reinforced escalation as effective. Even institutional challenge often

173

strengthened the internal narrative of persecution rather than prompting recalibration. Survival became proof of correctness.

Perhaps most striking is the continuity. From early business disputes to the presidency, the operating philosophy remained remarkably stable. Loyalty was prized. Critics were counterattacked. Institutions were tested. Adaptation, when it occurred, was tactical rather than psychological. Course correction was limited because reinforcement was constant.

Power, in theory, can refine leaders. It can expose blind spots and demand adjustment. In Trump's case, power magnified existing tendencies. Authority expanded the scale at which personality operated. Confidence hardened. Grievance deepened. The feedback loop between affirmation and escalation intensified.

Supporters interpret this consistency as strength—a refusal to bend to establishment pressure. Critics interpret it as rigidity—an inability to internalize institutional norms. Both readings acknowledge the same phenomenon: durability of character under stress.

The psychology of power is not abstract. It shapes decisions, relationships, and legacy. When reinforcement outpaces reflection, patterns become entrenched. When entrenched patterns meet global responsibility, consequences widen.

As we move into the next chapter, we turn from psychology to impact. Because personality and power are not ends in themselves. They produce outcomes—political, institutional, and cultural. And the final measure of leadership lies not only in how it was exercised, but in what it leaves behind.

Chapter 16: Legacy of a Temperament

In the end, presidencies are remembered not only for policies enacted or laws signed, but for the tone they set and the culture they leave behind. Donald Trump's time in power cannot be separated from the temperament that defined it. From business to television to the White House, personality was never peripheral. It was central. Now, as we assess legacy, the question is not simply what changed during his presidency—but what endured because of it.

This chapter examines the long shadow cast by a governing style rooted in confrontation, loyalty, grievance, and spectacle. Institutions were tested. Norms were stretched. Public trust shifted. Political discourse hardened. Supporters felt represented in ways they had not before. Critics felt alarmed in ways they had not anticipated. The emotional temperature of American politics rose and has yet to cool.

Legacy is complex. Trump reshaped the Republican Party, altered media dynamics, and redefined how campaigns operate in a digital age. He demonstrated the power of direct communication and base mobilization. He challenged traditional assumptions about political viability and elite gatekeeping. At the same time, he intensified polarization and deepened institutional strain.

Temperament, more than ideology, became the defining through-line. Sensitivity to criticism influenced response to oversight. Preference for dominance shaped negotiation. Escalation structured rhetoric. Survival reinforced instinct. The presidency became an extension of patterns visible long before it.

In this final chapter, we assess how a temperament—once confined to boardrooms and television studios—reverberated through constitutional structures. What happens to democratic culture when confrontation becomes normalized? How durable are the institutional changes introduced under pressure? And how will future leaders interpret the precedents set during this era?

Legacy is not fixed in the moment of departure. It unfolds over time. But temperament leaves imprint immediately. And in the case of Donald Trump, that imprint is inseparable from the personality that carried him to power.

Long-Term Effects on Political Discourse and Governance Norms

One of the most enduring elements of Donald Trump's presidency may not be a specific policy, but a transformation in tone. Political discourse in the United States shifted measurably during and after his time in office. Language that once lived on the fringes of political rhetoric moved toward the center. Confrontation became routine. Personal attack became normalized. The boundary between political disagreement and moral condemnation thinned.

Trump's style rewarded sharpness over subtlety. Social media amplified immediacy over deliberation. Slogans often replaced extended policy debate. Over time, this approach influenced not only his supporters, but also his critics. Political opponents adopted more combative framing in response. Cable news panels mirrored the intensity. The discourse ecosystem hardened across ideological lines.

The erosion of informal norms also marked a significant shift. Historically, presidents have clashed with the press and judiciary, but language questioning institutional legitimacy was comparatively restrained. Under Trump, describing the media as "fake" or institutions as corrupt became commonplace. The impact extended beyond his tenure. Skepticism toward mainstream media and federal agencies deepened among large segments of the electorate.

Governance norms likewise experienced strain. Expectations regarding transparency, conflict of interest boundaries, and executive communication shifted. Public disputes between the president and members of his own administration became routine. Rapid personnel turnover normalized instability within executive leadership. Direct communication via personal social media accounts altered traditional channels of public messaging.

Congressional dynamics changed as well. Party loyalty intensified. Primary challenges became more prominent enforcement mechanisms. The fear of public rebuke reshaped internal dissent. This recalibration of party discipline did not dissolve after Trump's presidency; it continued to influence candidate positioning and legislative behavior.

Perhaps most significantly, the perception of elections and institutional legitimacy became more polarized. Assertions about electoral integrity, amplified during and after the 2020 election, left lasting effects on public trust. Debates about certification processes, judicial review, and federal-state authority moved from technical procedure to emotional battleground.

Supporters argue that these shifts exposed underlying tensions long ignored by political elites. They contend that Trump did not create polarization but revealed it. Critics argue that his rhetoric and governing style accelerated fragmentation and weakened shared civic norms. Both interpretations acknowledge that the environment changed.

Political culture is resilient but not static. Norms evolve through precedent. When confrontational language becomes common, it lowers the threshold for future leaders to adopt similar tone. When institutions are framed as adversarial, public confidence becomes harder to restore. When spectacle dominates discourse, policy detail risks marginalization.

The long-term effects are still unfolding. Some changes may prove temporary reactions to an extraordinary presidency. Others may represent structural realignment in how American politics operates. What is clear is that temperament influenced trajectory. The tone of one presidency reverberated across branches, parties, and media landscapes.

Legacy, in this sense, extends beyond individual achievement. It shapes the operating culture of governance itself. And in that culture, the imprint of Trump's style remains visible—measured not only in policy outcomes, but in the language and norms that frame American political life.

Trump as Precedent Instead of Anomaly

In the immediate aftermath of Donald Trump's presidency, much commentary framed his rise as an anomaly—a disruption unlikely to recur. Yet as time passes, a different interpretation gains traction: Trump may represent not an exception to the system, but a precedent within it. The mechanisms that elevated him—media saturation, populist grievance, direct digital communication, party realignment—remain intact. In some respects, they have strengthened.

Trump demonstrated that traditional gatekeepers—party elites, major donors, editorial boards—no longer possess decisive control over candidate viability. A figure with strong command of attention and base loyalty can bypass institutional filters. That model has reshaped campaign strategy across parties. Candidates increasingly cultivate personal brand, social media dominance, and outsider rhetoric rather than rely solely on institutional endorsement.

The normalization of confrontational rhetoric also sets precedent. Language once considered politically disqualifying is now part of mainstream discourse. Future leaders, observing that sharp attack can mobilize loyal constituencies, may adopt similar strategies. The boundaries of acceptable political speech have shifted, not temporarily, but structurally.

Within party politics, Trump redefined leadership authority. Personal loyalty and alignment with a mobilized base proved more influential than traditional seniority or committee structure. This model of party dominance—leader-centered rather than institution-centered—offers a blueprint for others seeking similar control. The transformation of primary elections into mechanisms of ideological enforcement did not end with his tenure.

Governance practices also reflect precedent. Direct presidential communication through personal platforms is now normalized. Public disputes between executive and intelligence agencies, courts, or state officials have entered routine political vocabulary. Future administrations inherit not only the office, but the altered expectations surrounding it.

Perhaps most consequential is the precedent regarding institutional confrontation. Trump demonstrated that sustained rhetorical attack on oversight bodies can consolidate loyal support, even if it deepens polarization. The strategic framing of accountability as persecution has entered the political playbook. Whether future leaders use it as frequently is uncertain, but its viability has been tested.

Supporters argue that Trump expanded democratic participation by energizing voters who felt excluded. Critics contend that he lowered institutional guardrails and weakened trust. Both views acknowledge that the system adapted around him rather than rejecting him outright. Electoral success confers legitimacy. Legitimacy establishes precedent.

History often reframes disruptive figures as transitional rather than exceptional. The question is not whether Trump's presidency was unique—it was. The question is whether its operating principles will endure. Early indicators suggest that elements of his approach—media dominance, grievance mobilization, leader-centered party identity— have become embedded features of modern politics.

An anomaly fades. A precedent persists. Trump's impact lies not only in what he did, but in what he proved possible. The structural pathways he navigated remain open. And as long as those pathways exist, his presidency will function less as a deviation and more as a template within the evolving architecture of American political life.

How Personality Reshaped Institutional Expectations

Presidential institutions are designed to outlast individual occupants. Norms, protocols, and traditions create continuity even as leaders change. Yet during Donald Trump's presidency, personality did not simply operate within those expectations, it altered them. Over time, institutions adjusted not only to policy priorities, but to temperament.

One of the most visible shifts involved communication. The expectation that presidential messaging would move primarily through formal channels weakened. Agencies, foreign governments, and markets learned to monitor personal social media accounts as direct sources of executive signal. What had once been considered informal commentary became operational guidance. Future administrations inherit a communication environment where immediacy competes with deliberation as default.

Internal executive culture shifted as well. Rapid turnover normalized instability at senior levels. Public dismissal of cabinet officials became less shocking. The idea that high-ranking advisers might learn of removal through media announcements, once extraordinary, entered precedent. Institutional durability absorbed personalization.

Congressional expectations also evolved. Lawmakers recalibrated behavior in response to visible public rebuke or endorsement. Primary elections became more central tools of discipline. Party leadership roles increasingly required visible alignment with a central figure. Even critics of Trump adjusted strategy to operate within the climate he shaped.

Judicial and investigative institutions adapted in parallel. Courts anticipated public criticism and security concerns tied to high-profile rulings. Inspectors general and career officials operated within a context of heightened scrutiny and politicization. Oversight continued, but under new rhetorical pressure.

Diplomatic norms felt impact as well. Foreign leaders engaged not only with policy substance but with public tone. Alliances were managed amid uncertainty about messaging consistency. Personal rapport sometimes carried as much visible weight as institutional continuity.

Perhaps most significantly, public expectations shifted. Voters became accustomed to heightened rhetorical intensity and continuous confrontation. The threshold for political controversy rose. Actions that might once have defined an administration became routine headlines. Institutions proved resilient, but their surrounding cultural assumptions changed.

Supporters argue that these shifts democratized power by reducing elite mediation. Critics argue that they weakened guardrails and blurred boundaries between office and individual. Regardless of perspective, the imprint of personality is measurable.

Institutional expectations are shaped not only by written law but by lived example. When precedent expands the range of acceptable conduct, that expansion rarely contracts fully. Future leaders will operate within a presidency recalibrated by visibility, personalization, and confrontation.

Personality, in this sense, becomes institutional architecture. It defines not only how power is exercised, but how it is anticipated. Under Trump, institutions did not collapse. They adapted. And adaptation, once established, reshapes the operating environment long after the individual has left the stage.

The Imprint of Temperament

By the end of this final chapter, the central theme of this book comes into focus. Donald Trump's legacy cannot be understood solely through policy achievements or electoral outcomes. It must be understood through temperament. From business to the presidency, personality shaped approach. In office, that personality reshaped expectation.

Political discourse hardened. Confrontation normalized. Institutions absorbed sustained rhetorical pressure. Party structures recalibrated around leader-centered authority. Communication channels accelerated and personalized. The press, the courts, Congress, and even executive agencies adjusted to a presidency that operated through immediacy and dominance rather than institutional ritual.

Trump proved that a leader could bypass traditional gatekeepers, mobilize grievance into political force, and maintain loyalty through constant narrative conflict. In doing so, he altered assumptions about viability and endurance. Whether viewed as disruption or democratization, the precedent remains.

The long arc of this study reveals remarkable consistency. Early patterns of control, escalation, image sensitivity, and retaliation did not dissipate under the weight of office. They scaled. Success reinforced instinct. Survival validated method. Course correction was limited because reinforcement was frequent.

Temperament became legacy. Not simply because it was controversial, but because it endured. Institutions proved resilient, but they did not remain untouched. Norms stretched. Boundaries shifted. Public trust fragmented along partisan lines.

History will continue to debate the balance sheet of this era. Supporters will point to economic performance, judicial appointments, and foreign policy posture. Critics will point to polarization, institutional strain, and rhetorical division. Both sides will interpret impact through their own frameworks. But beneath policy dispute lies something more elemental: the imprint of a personality that refused to separate identity from authority.

In the end, Donald Trump did not simply occupy the presidency. He redefined its tone. And tone, once altered at that level, reverberates beyond a single term. The legacy of a temperament is not confined to years in office. It lingers in expectations, in discourse, and in the architecture of political possibility itself.

CONCLUSION

Understanding the Man to Understand the Moment

By the end of this final chapter, the central theme of this book comes into focus. Donald Trump's legacy cannot be understood solely through policy achievements or electoral outcomes. It must be understood through temperament. From business to the presidency, personality shaped approach. In office, that personality reshaped expectation.

Political discourse hardened. Confrontation normalized. Institutions absorbed sustained rhetorical pressure. Party structures recalibrated around leader-centered authority. Communication channels accelerated and personalized. The press, the courts, Congress, and even executive agencies adjusted to a presidency that operated through immediacy and dominance rather than institutional ritual.

Trump proved that a leader could bypass traditional gatekeepers, mobilize grievance into political force, and maintain loyalty through constant narrative conflict. In doing so, he altered assumptions about viability and endurance. Whether viewed as disruption or democratization, the precedent remains.

The long arc of this study reveals remarkable consistency. Early patterns of control, escalation, image sensitivity, and retaliation did not dissipate under the weight of office. They scaled. Success reinforced instinct. Survival validated method. Course correction was limited because reinforcement was frequent.

Temperament became legacy. Not simply because it was controversial, but because it endured. Institutions proved resilient, but they did not remain untouched. Norms stretched. Boundaries shifted. Public trust fragmented along partisan lines.

History will continue to debate the balance sheet of this era. Supporters will point to economic performance, judicial appointments, and foreign policy posture. Critics will point to polarization, institutional strain, and rhetorical division. Both sides will interpret impact through their own frameworks. But beneath policy dispute lies something more elemental: the imprint of a personality that refused to separate identity from authority.

In the end, Donald Trump did not simply occupy the presidency. He redefined its tone. And tone, once altered at that level, reverberates beyond a single term. The legacy of a temperament is not confined to years in office. It lingers in expectations, in discourse, and in the architecture of political possibility itself.

Reiterating the Value of Historical Continuity

As we conclude this work, it is essential to return to the principle that has guided it from the beginning: historical continuity matters. Donald Trump did not emerge suddenly in 2015 as a fully formed political phenomenon. The patterns visible in his presidency—confrontation, grievance, dominance, image-consciousness, loyalty enforcement— were present decades earlier in business dealings, media strategy, and legal conflicts. To understand the presidency, we had to understand the person. To understand the person, we had to trace the pattern.

Too often, political analysis isolates moments. A speech is examined. A crisis is dissected. An election is interpreted in isolation. But history does not operate in fragments. It operates in trajectories. The businessman who fought contractors publicly is connected to the president who fought institutions publicly. The television figure who performed decisive authority is connected to the candidate who promised unilateral strength. The litigant who escalated disputes is connected to the leader who framed oversight as persecution.

Continuity does not mean inevitability. It means context. By examining Trump's past actions and repeated behavioral patterns, we move beyond surface-level explanation. We see reinforcement over time. We see survival shaping instinct. We see how environments rewarded certain traits and discouraged introspection. That through-line is critical, because it transforms what might appear as episodic controversy into coherent narrative.

Historical continuity also clarifies the broader lesson: institutions respond not only to ideology, but to temperament. The presidency is influenced by the occupant's history. Patterns that go unchallenged in earlier arenas become magnified in higher office. When escalation repeatedly succeeds, it becomes strategy. When loyalty enforcement consolidates power, it becomes governance method.

This perspective resists sensationalism. It does not rely on surprise. It observes accumulation. The traits that defined Trump's rise were not hidden. They were documented, reported, and often celebrated long before they carried constitutional weight. The presidency did not invent them; it inherited them.

Reiterating continuity is not about assigning blame. It is about understanding causation. Political systems do not generate leaders in a vacuum. They elevate individuals whose traits resonate with cultural and institutional conditions of their time. By tracing Trump's continuity, we also trace the evolution of media, party politics, and public trust that made his ascent possible.

In the end, historical continuity grounds analysis. It prevents mythmaking. It replaces shock with pattern recognition. And it reminds us that leadership, especially at the highest level, is rarely transformation without precedent. It is amplification of what already exists.

To understand the present, we must follow the thread backward. Only then can we fully grasp how personality, power, and history converged in this era—and how their convergence will shape what comes next.

Why Trump's Negative and Eccentric Traits are Not Sudden Developments

A central argument of this book is that Donald Trump's most controversial traits did not appear abruptly during his presidency. They were not products of political pressure alone, nor sudden reactions to opposition. They were long-standing characteristics visible across decades—sometimes overlooked, sometimes rewarded, often reframed as strengths rather than liabilities.

In the 1970s and 1980s, accounts from contractors, attorneys, and business partners already described patterns of aggressive negotiation, public counterattack, and personal sensitivity to criticism. Legal disputes were escalated rather than quietly settled. Image management was constant. Critics were confronted directly. These behaviors were documented long before national politics entered the picture.

In the 1990s, during financial crisis and debt renegotiation, the same tendencies surfaced. Rather than retreat from public visibility after near insolvency, Trump amplified it. Confidence was projected even amid structural instability. Responsibility was often reframed. Survival reinforced the approach. What some described as denial or deflection, others interpreted as resilience.

The television era further normalized eccentric traits. On *The Apprentice*, dominance was theatricalized. Public humiliation became entertainment. Decisiveness—real or edited—was rewarded with ratings. The format did not correct impulsiveness; it elevated it. The persona hardened because it worked.

When Trump entered politics, those established patterns simply migrated arenas. The combative style used in business disputes became rally rhetoric. The instinct to litigate became the instinct to investigate critics. The fixation on loyalty in corporate environments became loyalty expectation within government. The adversarial stance toward media carried over seamlessly.

It is tempting to view the presidency as a turning point, a moment when character changed under strain. But the evidence suggests continuity rather than rupture. Traits labeled eccentric in office were visible in interviews decades earlier. Sensitivity to perceived disrespect was not new. The impulse to escalate rather than concede was not new. The preference for spectacle over detail was not new.

What changed was scale. Private eccentricity became public governance. Personal grievance became national narrative. The structural environment shifted from boardroom to White House, but the psychological patterns did not.

Recognizing this continuity matters. It challenges the notion that crisis alone produced volatility. It suggests instead that reinforcement over time solidified behavioral reflexes. Success did not moderate traits; it validated them. The presidency did not invent personality. It amplified it.

Supporters may interpret these enduring traits as authenticity—evidence that Trump remained consistent under pressure. Critics see them as warning signs that were long visible but insufficiently weighed. Either way, the claim that these characteristics emerged suddenly under political stress does not align with the historical record.

In understanding Trump's leadership, we must resist narratives of sudden transformation. The arc is cumulative. The traits were there from the beginning – visible, documented, reinforced. What changed was not their presence, but their consequence.

The Importance of Evidence-Based Personality Analysis in Political Leadership

Political leadership is often evaluated through ideology, policy outcomes, or electoral success. Yet personality is not secondary to those measures, it is foundational. The way a leader responds to criticism, handles pressure, interprets loyalty, and manages impulse shapes decision-making at every level. For this reason, evidence-based personality analysis is not an indulgence. It is a necessary tool of political understanding.

Evidence-based analysis does not rely on speculation or armchair diagnosis. It draws from documented behavior across time: interviews, recorded statements, firsthand accounts from associates, observable patterns of response to stress, and repeated decision-making habits. In the case of Donald Trump, decades of public record provide a substantial behavioral archive. Patterns visible in business disputes, media engagements, campaign rhetoric, and presidential conduct create continuity that can be examined systematically.

Understanding personality matters because leadership is exercised under pressure. Crisis reveals reflex. Negotiation reveals temperament. Oversight reveals tolerance for constraint. If a leader consistently escalates under challenge, that pattern will likely recur in diplomacy. If a leader equates dissent with disloyalty, internal governance will reflect it. If a leader seeks affirmation intensely, communication strategy will be shaped accordingly.

Evidence-based personality analysis also helps avoid mythmaking. Leaders are often cast as either heroic reformers or dangerous aberrations. Neither caricature captures the complexity of human behavior. Careful analysis grounded in documented conduct allows observers to distinguish between isolated incidents and structural tendencies.

In democratic systems, voters evaluate not only promises but judgment. Judgment is inseparable from personality. The capacity for restraint, empathy, adaptability, and introspection influences how power is wielded. Conversely, rigidity, hypersensitivity, or retaliatory instinct can shape institutional friction. These are not abstract qualities—they produce measurable outcomes.

Critics sometimes argue that personality analysis risks reducing politics to psychology. But the opposite is true when done responsibly. It integrates psychology with context. It recognizes that institutions interact with individuals. A constitutional framework is resilient, but it is not immune to the temperament of those who operate within it.

In the modern media environment, where leaders communicate directly and constantly, personality is more visible than ever. The digital age compresses reaction time. Impulse can become policy signal. Emotional tone can move markets. The psychological dimension of leadership has never been more consequential.

In the case examined throughout this book, patterns were not inferred from isolated events. They were drawn from decades of repeated behavior—responses to crisis, management of dissent, interaction with institutions, handling of scrutiny. That longitudinal perspective strengthens analysis and reduces conjecture.

Ultimately, evidence-based personality analysis serves a civic purpose. It encourages voters, scholars, and institutions to evaluate leadership beyond surface rhetoric. It asks not only what a leader promises, but how that leader has historically behaved when challenged. It invites scrutiny of continuity, reinforcement, and adaptation.

Political systems are shaped by laws and norms, but they are animated by people. To ignore personality is to ignore a central variable of governance. To analyze it responsibly is not to personalize politics, it is to understand it more fully.

Final Reflection: Informed Citizenship over Reactionary Judgment

As we close this book, one principle stands above all others: democratic strength depends not on reaction, but on reflection. Political eras defined by intensity and confrontation invite emotional response. Outrage becomes immediate. Loyalty becomes reflexive. Judgment becomes instantaneous. Yet democracy is sustained not by speed, but by informed citizenship.

Donald Trump's rise and presidency unfolded in an age of constant stimulus—social media alerts, breaking news banners, viral clips, and perpetual commentary. In such an environment, reaction can eclipse understanding. Supporters react defensively. Critics react indignantly. Nuance disappears in the exchange. But governance demands more than reflex.

Informed citizenship requires historical perspective. It asks citizens to examine patterns, not just moments. It asks them to evaluate consistency over time rather than isolated controversy. It encourages analysis of evidence—documented behavior, institutional response, long-term consequence—rather than viral impression.

This is not a call for neutrality in moral judgment. Citizens are entitled to strong views. It is a call for discipline in forming those views. Reactionary judgment thrives on immediacy and emotional charge. Informed judgment requires patience and evidence. It separates loyalty from critical thinking. It distinguishes disagreement from hostility. It evaluates leadership not solely by rhetoric, but by pattern.

The story traced in this book illustrates how personality, power, media, and institutions intersect. It also demonstrates how public response shapes outcome. Leaders rise not only through personal ambition, but through cultural conditions that reward certain traits. Those conditions are influenced by citizen engagement—what we amplify, what we tolerate, what we question.

Democracy is not weakened by scrutiny. It is weakened by indifference or blind allegiance. Informed citizenship means examining leaders critically without dehumanizing them. It means resisting caricature while acknowledging documented behavior. It means demanding accountability without surrendering to perpetual outrage.

In the end, the health of a republic depends less on any single presidency than on the civic habits of its people. Reaction sustains polarization. Reflection sustains stability. Reaction magnifies spectacle. Reflection strengthens institutions.

The era examined in these pages will be debated for decades. Interpretations will differ sharply. But one enduring lesson remains: citizenship is not passive. It requires engagement grounded in evidence, awareness of history, and willingness to look beyond immediate emotion.

Power passes. Personalities rise and fall. Institutions endure when citizens approach them not with reflex, but with reason.

www.ingramcontent.com/pod-product-compliance
Lightning Source LLC
Chambersburg PA
CBHW070756160726
48004CB00001B/215